What people are saying about *Renovated for Glory*

Landen Dorsch's, *Renovated for Glory*, is a great book, balanced, biblical, interesting, and addresses current issues and concerns of the Church. You will be educated, enlightened, encouraged, and edified by reading it. I consider Landen a good friend, and a gifted pastor and communicator. He has been with me several times on ministry trips around the world, and has helped me minister to sometimes thousands in a service. He writes not from the ivory tower of academia, but from the trenches of local church ministry. He values the glory. I recommend Landen and *Renovated for Glory* to anyone who wants to learn more about living in the glory of God.

Randy Clark
D. Min. Th.D.
Overseer of the Apostolic Network of Global Awakening
founder of Global Awakening.

In his book *Renovated for Glory*, Landen Dorsch beautifully illuminates his revelation of what it means to be transformed by the renewal our minds so that we can be acceptable and profitable in the service of the King. This is not a book about religion or rules but about relationship. He has successfully constructed for us the foundational truths and pillars that are necessary for us to operate powerfully under an open heaven.

We have known Landen for years, as a man of character and honor. Most teachers unveil principles; Landen, because he has lived what he is teaching, is able to impart life. This is a book of substance and we recommend it for those who want to go deeper and further in the Kingdom. The Pillar prayers and confessions at the end of the chapters drive home the power of activating, not just learning, the truths revealed. Enjoy the read; it will change the way you think!

Ken & Jeanne Harrington
Authors and international conference speakers
Co-founders of Treasure Chest Ministries
Co-founders of Nabin Life Care Centre

Pastor Landen Dorsch has been like a spiritual son to me for close to 30 years. Watching him grow in grace and truth has been such a delight. The Bible is God's word unto salvation and is filled with divine direction. Understanding the freedom that is available to each of us is amazing. The teaching on how you and I can have a renewed mind, according to Romans 12:2, is one of the most important discoveries in scripture. I believe this book will help shape your destiny as you allow the Word of God to reveal the freedom that Christ has for you NOW!

Rev. Ken Solbrekken
ABNWT District Superintendent of the PAOC

Rev. Landen Dorsch has been my pastor and a spiritual father to me for 20 years. I have always been amazed at how he creates powerful language that paints a mental picture to communicate deep spiritual revelation. Anyone who reads this book needs to commit to the journey. It's not light reading, but it is deeply transformational. Whether part of his pastoral team or as a congregation member, these word pictures stick in our minds and enable us to apply life transforming revelation on a both a corporate and personal level.

Amy Ball
Children's Pastor
Gateway Family Church

There is a move of the Spirit happening even as we speak. Many leaders are receiving fresh revelation in order to prepare God's people to fully enter into and participate in a move of God. Landen is one of those leaders, and *Renovated for Glory* is one of those books. We are in a time when we need to be listening to what leaders are receiving. I will often begin the reading of a book because it is based on a dream or a vision, but to sustain reading to the end I am looking for interpretation and application for real life. My friend Landen brings the revelation he has received from God all the way home. Read and be made ready!

Dr. Kim Maas
Itinerant Minister/Speaker
@pkmaas / www.kimmaas.com

I have had the privilege of being under Landen's leadership for the last nine years. His father's heart is evident in his leadership, his teaching and his writing. He is a passionate leader that loves to see people walk in the fullness of who God has created them to be. This book offers a unique perspective on how changing where you think from can set you free from past strongholds and equip you for an incredible future.

Paul Drader
Executive Pastor
Gateway Family Church

For years Landen and I have talked about his book writing and what amazing quotes should be inside it! *Renovated for Glory* is not a collection of quotes and stories, instead it is an expression of a transformed heart. Landen is a leader who shares what he has learned out of revelation from God and His word. The six pillars that Landen shares are themes that he has personally experienced and lived out with his family, his church and his friendships. You will find yourself inspired as you read and will probably want to hunt Landen down for a coffee to talk deeply about being transformed by Jesus. I encourage you to pray before you read and ask God to speak to you personally. God did that for me, and I know He will do that for you.

Darcy McAllister
Personnel and Family Life Director for International
Missions in the Pentecostal Assemblies of Canada

Reverend Landen Dorsch is a gifted pastor of Gateway Family Church at Leduc AB, a growing church operating in signs and miracles. As a Missions Pastor I count it a real privilege and blessing to serve with him, and to see the expansion of God's kingdom.

Pastor Landen has a heart for missions, and has travelled with me to the Philippines doing crusades and Pastoral Leadership Conferences. He was mightily used by God to bring encouragement to pastors and their congregations, many of whom experienced the supernatural power of God.

Renovated for Glory is a life transforming book, encouraging you to seek the glory of an " open heaven." Every chapter is filled with significant teaching backed by the scriptures which makes it very riveting as you seek to understand and be transformed by God's glory.

After reading *Renovated for Glory* you will be encouraged to live and walk victoriously, equipped to understand and address current common issues of concern to the church.

I highly recommend Pastor Landen's book for a broader understanding of embracing the Supernatural.

Rev. Mohan Maharaj
Missions Pastor, Gateway Family Church
Leduc, Alberta. Canada.
President of Global Ministries.
President of Aspire Group Realty Inc.
Edmonton, Alberta.

I have waited with great expectancy for this book to be written. For many years I have had the privilege of listening to Landen teach. His wisdom has helped form how I see myself, my God and those around me. I have often gone back to Landen's teachings and have always found more each time. I believe this book will be another great resource to those who are hungry, those who are curious and those who want more of God. It is a book which I will proudly host in my library and one which I will return to often.

Kayle Mumby
Prophetic Overseer, Gateway Family Church
Itinerant Minister/Speaker
www.kaylemumby.com

If there is one thing that this emerging generation is looking for, it is "authenticity". Landen Dorsch in his book entitled *Renovated for Glory*, shares his message from a heart of honesty and transparency that rings true. We can identify with him as he leads us through a journey of discovery of "the six ancient pillars" that God has given us to be able to live under an open heaven!

Having known and loved Landen and his family for many years, I can confirm that in true apostolic form, he lays a foundation from the Word and with his own testimony that is unshakable.

I challenge you to pick up this book and read it. Test it. Prove it. I am confident that the same truth that has caused Landen to be free, will impact you as well.

In a world where too many Christians are tired, broken, outdated, or just plain irrelevant, it is time for us to be Renovated... for Glory!

Dennis Wiedrick

Landen Dorsch has been my pastor, mentor and friend for 20 years. There are few people on the planet that I love and trust more. We have journeyed together through many seasons of life and ministry spending countless hours processing and discerning our ideas about God and how He works in us. Landen's heart has always been to father a generation into wholeness and transformation, empowered to live fruitful and supernatural lives that reflect Christ's true humanity. *Renovated for Glory* brings language and imagery to the believers journey of transformation. It is an essential companion to anyone longing to discover their true identity and how it is firmly seated and secure in the finished works of Jesus. The world needs sons and daughters, filled with God himself, establishing His kingdom on the earth... The world needs a church that is *Renovated for Glory*.

Josh Frey
Associate and Worship Pastor
Gateway Family Church

Renovated
for GLORY

be So blessed!!

Renovated for GLORY

Renew Your Mind, Transform Your Life

Landen Dorsch

RENOVATED FOR GLORY
Copyright © 2016 by Landen Dorsch

Unless otherwise indicated, all scripture quotations are from the ESV® Bible (The Holy Bible, English Standard Version®), copyright © 2001 by Crossway, a publishing ministry of Good News Publishers. Used by permission. All rights reserved. Scripture quotations marked (NASB) taken from the New American Standard Bible® (NASB), Copyright © 1960, 1962, 1963, 1968, 1971, 1972, 1973, 1975, 1977, 1995 by The Lockman Foundation. Used by permission. www. Lockman.org. Scripture quotations taken from the Amplified® Bible (AMPC), Copyright © 1954, 1958, 1962, 1964, 1965, 1987 by The Lockman Foundation. Used by permission. www.Lockman.org. Scripture quotations from THE MESSAGE. Copyright © by Eugene H. Peterson 1993, 1994, 1995, 1996, 2000, 2001, 2002. Used by permission of NavPress. All rights reserved. Represented by Tyndale House Publishers, Inc. Scripture quotations marked (KJV) taken from the Holy Bible, King James Version, which is in the public domain.

Printed in Canada

ISBN: 978-1-4866-1428-8

Word Alive Press
131 Cordite Road, Winnipeg, MB R3W 1S1
www.wordalivepress.ca

MIX
Paper from responsible sources
FSC
www.fsc.org FSC® C016245

WORD ALIVE
—PRESS—

Library and Archives Canada Cataloguing in Publication

Dorsch, Landen, author
     Renovated for glory : renew your mind, transform your life / Landen Dorsch.

Issued in print and electronic formats.
ISBN 978-1-4866-1428-8 (softcover).--ISBN 978-1-4866-1429-5 (ebook)

     1. Christian life. I. Title.

BV4501.3.D67 2016   248.4   C2016-907713-6
                                                 C2016-907714-4

Cathy, I love you forever...

Contents

Acknowledgements

I am so grateful to the many people who have been so gracious to me over the years as I have grown in ministry. This book is the result of the many relationships that have shaped my life. I want to thank all those who offered endorsements, and Mike Love for his friendship and for writing the foreword.

To my staff, thank you for your unwavering commitment to our journey. I love you. Let's keep building giants.

I also want to thank my family for their grace and support throughout our ministry adventure. Alyssa, Tyler, Amy-Lynn, and Jenna, you are my pride and joy. Dad loves you so much. I also thank my wife Cathy, who is the truest love of my life, my best friend, and the safest place in the world. Elwin and Gloria, thank you for loving me as a son. Thank you to my parents, Fred and Diana, for their unwavering love, support, and encouragement over the years. You are the very best. Gram, thank you for your faithful intercession and love.

I am also so grateful for my Gateway family. I love being your pastor.

And of course I must thank Jesus, without whom none of this happens.

Foreword

I had coffee one day with a pastor who had just resigned from his church. He explained to me that even though he was the exiting leader, he had been tasked with helping his church find a suitable replacement. He asked if I had any suggestions and immediately I said, "Hold on, I know someone."

Right there, I pulled out my phone and called a friend. The outgoing pastor had no idea what I was doing or who I was calling. When my friend answered the phone, I began with these words: "You have been in the wilderness too long, my friend. The Lord has a new plan for you." This is something I'd said to him in a previous ministry transition. Then I handed the phone over to the pastor and they began the interview process.

The pastor of that church today is the author of this book, and his journey has been much like yours and mine—ever trusting, ever leaning, ever praying, ever desiring more revelation, pursuing the heart of the Father, having a healthy dissatisfaction for the way things are, and possessing a pure desire for the way things could be.

My first encounter with Landen Dorsch came when he was a youth director in central Alberta. I was so impressed with his passion to get into schools and reach out to young people. One of the ways he reached out to youth was through the local high school choir, which consisted not only of kids from his church but kids from the community. He taught them to sing worship songs even though the majority of those students were unchurched. It was one of several creative techniques Landen used to get the gospel into the lives of young people. His efforts left me intrigued, and I realized there was something special about this young man.

I've had the privilege to watch him grow through the years from being a youth pastor, then the executive director of a first-class outreach camp that specifically targeted at-risk teens, and then the lead pastor of Gateway Family Church. Through each transition, his heart has consistently longed after God and His kingdom purposes.

Today I see him as an incredible leader who refuses to settle for what's good enough, as so many believers have settled for in their own journeys. Landen reminds us all that we don't have to plateau in our relationship with God; we can freely pursue Him to the deep waters of intimacy. He calls us to live for Him with renewed minds and renovated hearts to see His glory manifested daily.

I would suggest that the starting point of being renovated for glory has less to do with doing something and more to do with being somewhere. I know for a fact that the "somewhere" for Landen has been his habit of wandering off into the quiet places, being still, and intimately knowing who God is. That's where we should all start.

I love this book firstly because I deeply admire several things about the author. He is authentic, a true believer, highly likeable, and a genuine friend. He and I have discussed many times that in life and leadership no one should ever walk alone. Wolves survive because they hunt and travel in packs. Landen is one of the trusted people in my pack. It is imperative that you surround yourself with friends who have your back, encourage you in your struggles, celebrate your victories, and hold you accountable for your choices.

I also love this book because it reminds me that God's presence is everything. It challenges me to never settle for second best when the best (His presence) is available. Never prioritize what you do over the One you do it for. I must confess that I've been guilty of knowing the work of the Lord more intimately than I knew the Lord of the work. Landen reminds us, "There is a new call to the body of Christ today. It's a call to value His presence over every other thing. No amount of work can make up for the lack of His presence." His presence is boss!

Foreword

I love this book for the practical and pastoral way Landen leads us through the scriptures and leaves us with a practical application which he calls renovated thoughts, glorified responses, pillar confessions, and pillar prayers. Reading through each of these will remind you that God is for you and is committed to revealing His glory in and through you.

It is a well-known fact in my house that I am a slow eater at mealtime. I'm not painfully slow, but I proceed at a pace that compliments the chef. I remind my wife that food is to be experienced, enjoyed, and appreciated. She simply reminds me to load the dishwasher when I'm done! This book should not be a speed read, like someone racing through a fast food eatery. It should be consumed slowly and attentively, pen and highlighter in hand, digesting every morsel, thought, and scripture that is shared so as to appreciate the heart and passion behind these pages.

As you read this book, I'm convinced that it will lead you from ordinary to extraordinary, something we were all designed for.

And we all, with unveiled face, beholding the glory of the Lord, are being transformed into the same image from one degree of glory to another. For this comes from the Lord who is the Spirit.
—2 Corinthians 3:18

That is why we never give up. Though our bodies are dying, our spirits are being renewed every day. For our present troubles are small and won't last very long. Yet they produce for us a glory that vastly outweighs them and will last forever!
—2 Corinthians 4:16–17, NLT

Simply put, my good friend has put on these pages what God has put in his heart. These wonderful insights will help us get from where we are to where we need to be—renovated for His glory.

Mike Love
Extreme Dream Ministries

Introduction

I want more.

That cry rings from the hearts of many people. No matter who or where they are, no matter how much or how little they have, humans are made with a unique craving to get more. More of what? Well, the short answer is God. The lived-out answer is expressed in all sorts of ways— money, fame, food, sex, drugs, time, vacations, pleasure, materials, objects... you name it, we want more of it. It's like we can't ever be satisfied with what we have.

It's an insatiable hunger, an inner urgency for more.

What if I told you that this hunger is a good thing? What if I told you that we were created with this hunger? What if it was God's idea?

> *He has made everything beautiful in its time. Also,* he has put eternity into man's heart, *yet so that he cannot find out what God has done from the beginning to the end.*
>
> —Ecclesiastes 3:11 (emphasis added)

That little phrase—*"he has put eternity into man's heart"*—is the source of our hunger. The next phrase shows us that the hunger will never end. The thing is, we don't hunger for temporal things. Unfortunately, we have been tricked by the enemy to *think* that temporal things will satisfy us, but they don't; they only provide a moment of pleasure for the senses.

Temporal things will never be able to satiate a hunger that's rooted in eternal things. And that is where human's hunger is seated. Eternity is hidden in our hearts.

We were made to search for God, but it doesn't end there. Our search starts in looking for God. But finding Him isn't the end, and that's when our craving nature, our inner hunger, becomes an amazing asset. Our hungry hearts get to search the infinite. We can forever love Him, search Him, discover Him, and experience Him—and our hunger empowers us to continue loving Him, searching Him, discovering Him, and experiencing Him. We get to be forever hungry for a forever God.

When The Honeymoon Is Over

Ahh, the wonder of young love! Many of us have experienced it. Most of us have seen and been amused by it.

In my ministry, I have performed many weddings and spent many, many hours counselling young couples prior to their weddings. Their generally rose-coloured lenses of marriage are amusing. I counsel them that there will be days when they'll have to work at love. In shock, they respond, "Oh that would never be us."

Like I said, it's amusing.

In Ephesians 5, Paul discusses how to develop and maintain a healthy marriage. But he also describes the relationship that the covenant of marriage reflects, which is the covenant of salvation that Jesus brought us into.

> *"Therefore a man shall leave his father and mother and hold fast to his wife, and the two shall become one flesh." This mystery is profound, and I am saying that it refers to Christ and the church.*
> —Ephesians 5:31–32

Marriage is a wonderful covenant. It's meant to be fulfilling, safe, encouraging, secure, and of course loving. But for those of us who have been working at marriage for a while, we also know that it's hard work.

Let's face it: marriage isn't one long passionate honeymoon. The sheen of young love wears off and becomes the reality of day-to-day cohabitation. We have to put in a lot of sacrifice, pain, work, and energy to maintain a healthy marriage.

You see, the entrance into marriage is emotional. Love, in its immaturity, is generally based on feelings. Those feelings are wonderful and very real, but they need to grow. The time, effort, and expense you spend on or with that special someone is initially based on how that someone makes you feel. In the early stages, this emotional form of love, or *eros* (the sensual form of love), has more to do with our individual return from the relationship than the cost of loving that person. As our love matures to *agape* (covenant love), we move beyond the feelings we experience *from* the relationship and bring life *to* the relationship.

In the same way, our early relationship with Jesus is somewhat like the honeymoon phase. We enter into the covenant emotionally and it's wonderful and very real. But the sheen of our first love wears off and we are faced with a choice.

The first option is to chase after God by going from place to place, hoping we will experience Him again and regain that feeling. The second option is to become disappointed and confused, wondering why we no longer feel Him but religiously continue on our journey. When the sheen of our first love with Jesus wears off, we're confronted with the immaturity of our *eros* and are given the opportunity to engage *agape*.

Now, a healthy marriage isn't meant to regress into a business partnership. We are meant to continue to know the passion that is given to us by God. And we are meant to know the power and wonder of a relationship that cannot be shaken because it isn't founded in feelings but rather covenant. Jesus spoke of this:

> *And then will I declare to them, "I never knew you; depart from me, you workers of lawlessness."*
> —Matthew 7:23

The word he used for "knew" is the Greek word *ginosko*, which means both an intellectual knowledge and an intimate knowledge.

I know my wife intellectually. I know what our relationship means, what it is, how it works, and how it grows. And I am secure in that knowledge. But I also have the wonder of knowing her intimately. She remains my one and only lover, and I continue to passionately enjoy all the wonderful feelings of love given to me in our covenant.

With Jesus, we are given the same relationship dynamic of knowing Him, experiencing the wonder of His touch, and pursuing the wonder of His infinite nature.

Love makes us hungry for more.

And that's where I found myself in February 2012. Wanting more. I needed to engage the search, to recalibrate my heart so I could lean into His infinite ways yet again.

The fear of the Lord is the beginning of wisdom, and the knowledge of the Holy One is insight.

—Proverbs 9:10

I was leading a healthy church. God had been moving powerfully. We had seen many miracles, and worship was intense and authentic. We were establishing a sense of family in the congregation, as well as a kingdom of heaven culture. This was an exciting time of growth both spiritually and numerically. We were becoming a people of His presence and seeing the results of that lifestyle manifested in freedom and liberty. What a wonderful season!

Even though the season was wonderful, every leader feels the responsibility to move forward. I've heard it said that good shepherds feed their flock in one pasture while looking over the hill for the next. That's where I was. I knew that we needed something more. We needed to refine the search and recalibrate our hearts.

Of the several definitions for calibrate goes like this: "to plan or devise (something) carefully so as to have a precise use, application, appeal, etc."[1]

---

1 *Dictionary.com*, "Calibrate." Date of access: November 1, 2016 (http://www.dictionary.com/browse/calibrate).

Once again, I was planning carefully, precisely. That's why I was recalibrating.

Recalibration doesn't have to be painful; it can be glorious. Times of wondrous worship and tears, laughter and silence. It's a wonder to pursue the amazing King of all kings!

...that the God of our Lord Jesus Christ, the Father of glory, may give you the Spirit of wisdom and of revelation in the knowledge of him, having the eyes of your hearts enlightened, that you may know what is the hope to which he has called you, what are the riches of his glorious inheritance in the saints, and what is the immeasurable greatness of his power toward us who believe, according to the working of his great might...

—Ephesians 1:17–19

Evon Horton once said that great leaders know where they are and know where they are headed. I knew where we were, but I wanted to know where God was steering us. We cannot lead without a clear sense of direction, and the source of that direction is God.

I would like to deviate for just a moment to submit a thought to you. I don't feel that vision should be birthed out of need alone. Even the world can see a need and answer it. We are not of this world. Jesus chastised His followers with this thought when He addressed the nature of His Father:

If you then, who are evil, know how to give good gifts to your children, how much more will your Father who is in heaven give good things to those who ask him!

—Matthew 7:11

Jesus said that even the evil among us know how to give good gifts. What separates our vision from the visions of the world is the revelation of God. I believe that vision is best birthed out of catching the heart of God, and His nature is revealed through the vision that's implemented.

How do we find out the vision? Proverbs 25:2 says, *"It is the glory of God to conceal things, but the glory of kings is to search things out."*

Our Father speaks differently to each of us. One of the first and most important lessons for the disciple is learning how to engage the Lord in intimacy, and through His Word discover how He speaks to you. He will not always speak the same way; you will learn to recognize His voice better in different forms when you know what He sounds like through familiarity. Our smaller faith steps lead to the clarity of knowing the voice of God so we are able to take larger steps later.

> One of the first and most important lessons for the disciple is learning how to engage the Lord in intimacy, and through His Word discover how He speaks to you.

For me, He often speaks in pictures. I'll see a vision of something and then He'll engage me in a game of hide and seek. He hides and I seek. He shows me a clue and, because of my curious nature, I embark on a pursuit of discovery.

This is what He did for me in my moment of recalibration. I suddenly saw in my spirit the image of an ancient Greek structure. It had a circular foundation with pillars all around it, but no roof overtop. I'm sure you have seen pictures of Greek structures. Because of the ancient nature of the structure, the white pillars gently contrasted against the cloud-darkened sky.

I saw a woman whom I knew to be from my church, although I couldn't recognize who it was. She entered the structure and knelt to pray. As she prayed, the clouds opened and a shaft of light filled the interior. Then I heard the Lord say to me, "There are ancient pillars that hold up an open heaven."

And so the pursuit began.

Introduction

This is a painting that is displayed in the sanctuary at Gateway Family Church.
I commissioned my sister Tangie Shields, who oversees the prophetic art
community at Gateway, to paint the vision I had of the pillars. To see
more of Tangie's work visit her Facebook page, Vibrant Artistry.

chapter one

Hooked

IN GOD'S TYPICAL WAY, HE HAD ME HOOKED: "THERE ARE ANCIENT PILLARS that hold up an open heaven."

I am continually amazed at God's poetic way of creating a word picture that is both beautiful and mysterious. Even more, I love how those word pictures can send me on a new pursuit of His goodness.

Questions and more questions. Questions like, what is an open heaven anyway? Why would something that is open need to be held up? What does He mean by ancient? These were just some of the queries racing through my mind.

"I've Closed the Door on That."

I've used that statement before. Perhaps you have as well. I've used it to say that while there was the potential of something happening, my choice was to end the possibility. Most of us at one time or another have closed the door on opportunities, relationships, purchases, and a myriad of other things.

There were two miraculous "openings" during Jesus' lifetime. The first was when He was baptized and the heavens were opened in the Gospels:

> *Now when all the people were baptized, and when Jesus also had been*
> *baptized and was praying, the heavens were opened, and the Holy*

Spirit descended on him in bodily form, like a dove; and a voice came from heaven, "You are my beloved Son; with you I am well pleased."

—Luke 3:21–22

At the moment of His baptism, God opened the heavens and the Holy Spirit came upon Him. It was at this point that the Lord opened up heaven for the world. Yes, others had "seen" into an open heaven, but here the Lord opened up the heavens and the Holy Spirit descended in the form of a dove. Jesus then became a gateway for heaven here on earth.

The Bible then says that He was led by the Spirit into the wilderness to be tempted, and upon returning He was filled with power. Then Jesus declared,

The Spirit of the Lord is upon me, because he has anointed me to proclaim good news to the poor. He has sent me to proclaim liberty to the captives and recovering of sight to the blind, to set at liberty those who are oppressed, to proclaim the year of the Lord's favor.

—Luke 4:18–19

He was saying, "The Son of Man is about to show you how to live like a son of God."

God opened the heavens and then Jesus modelled a lifestyle under an open heaven. By the way, it doesn't say that God ever closed the heavens. They remain open to us.

Upon Jesus' death, another prophetic demonstration of the openness of heaven was revealed in the tearing of the temple veil.

And behold, the curtain of the temple was torn in two, from top to bottom. And the earth shook, and the rocks were split. The tombs also were opened. And many bodies of the saints who had fallen asleep were raised, and coming out of the tombs after his resurrection they went into the holy city and appeared to many. When the centurion and those who were with him, keeping watch over Jesus, saw the earthquake and what took place, they were filled with awe and said, "Truly this was the Son of God!"

—Matthew 27:51–54

The temple veil separated the Most Holy place from the rest of the temple. The Most Holy Place, or Holy of Holies, was where the Ark of the Covenant was placed. This veil was part of the blueprint given to Moses when he was given the task of building the tabernacle. Its purpose was to separate mankind from God's holy presence. In a sense, it protected sinful man from a holy God. Imagine the shock of the Pharisees entering the temple after getting rid of this upstart Jesus, who claimed that He was the Messiah and that the kingdom of heaven was at hand, only to discover that the veil protecting them from the presence of God had been torn.

The message could not have been any clearer: there need not any longer be a separation between mankind and His manifest presence. The atonement had been made.

Therefore, brothers, since we have confidence to enter the holy places by the blood of Jesus, by the new and living way that he opened for us through the curtain, that is, through his flesh, and since we have a great priest over the house of God, let us draw near with a true heart in full assurance of faith, with our hearts sprinkled clean from an evil conscience and our bodies washed with pure water.

—Hebrews 10:19–22

What does this have to do with "closing the door"? God has opened heaven over us. However, much of mankind has closed the door on the possibility of living under that open heaven.

Put simply, living under an open heaven means having all of heaven's resources behind everything we do. It means living with the reality of His kingdom manifesting in everyday life. It's where the miraculous is normal, where the nature of the kingdom, which we are ambassadors of, is reflected in our lives (2 Corinthians 5:19–20).

So what does that look like?

Think of it from the perspective of realms. The first realm is a physical one which we'll call the temporal. This is the visible reality around us. It's the realm that we perceive with our senses. The second realm is spiritual, the atmosphere. This is the realm where the enemy presides as the prince of the power of the air (Ephesians 2:2). Lastly, there is a third realm which is also spiritual, the third heaven, where the Lord resides. Paul wrote of this in 2 Corinthians 12, describing his experience in the presence of the Lord. When Jesus prayed "Your kingdom come," He was praying that the reality of the third heaven, His realm, would be manifest in the temporal.

In between the temporal and third heaven is the second realm, the atmosphere, where the enemy clouds over mankind, interfering with the nature of heaven being experienced by man.

Then Jesus came and was baptized, fulfilling all righteousness. The heavens opened and the Holy Spirit descended on Him like a dove, tearing a hole in the second realm. Jesus then lived under an open heaven, having unfettered access to God's realm.

That's why the devil immediately tempted Jesus. He had to find some way to send cloud cover over Jesus to suspend the power and anointing that was going to come from heaven on Jesus' behalf.

Satan continues to do the same to us today.

In the same way that the Holy Spirit came on Christ, our baptism of the Holy Spirit releases to us the authority to command the second heaven to open, giving us unfettered access to the third heaven, our Father's kingdom.

> ...*so that* through the church the manifold wisdom of God might now be made known to the rulers and authorities in the heavenly places. *This was according to the eternal purpose that he has realized in Christ Jesus our Lord,* in whom we have boldness and access with confidence through our faith in him.
>
> —Ephesians 3:10–12 (emphasis added)

But what if it's still a little cloudy? In Ephesians 4:27, Paul counsels us not to give any place to the devil. Sometimes the open heaven we should be experiencing is clouded because of issues we have with ourselves. Always remember that God is perfect, so when the imperfect seems to be happening, the issue is never with Him. My point is that we're the ones being perfected; He already is perfect.

Therefore, we need to be aware that our ways of thinking in different areas of our lives have an impact on the manifestation of the openness of heaven. This is why we need to experience the renewal of our minds.

Renovated for Glory

Paul wrote to us in the book of Romans about being glorified.

For those whom he foreknew he also predestined to be conformed to the image of his Son, in order that he might be the firstborn among many brothers. And those whom he predestined he also called, and those whom he called he also justified, and those whom he justified he also glorified.

—Romans 8:29–30

We have a responsibility as believers to grow into glory. Many are satisfied with just being called. Many are satisfied with just being justified, or saved. But we are meant to also be glorified. That's what open heaven living looks like: the glory of God manifest here on earth.

It may sound dangerously arrogant or foolhardy to encourage people to live a glorified life. Perhaps that could lead to pride and arrogance. Jesus, however, modelled for us the way to manage the glory of God.

When Jesus had spoken these words, he lifted up his eyes to heaven, and said, "Father, the hour has come; glorify your Son that the Son may glorify you…"

—John 17:1

Recently, one of the board members of my church, John, shared this scripture with me and the amazing truth that's attached to it. Jesus said, "Father, glorify Me." That sounds like an arrogant statement, but the purpose of Him being glorified wasn't so that He could receive glory, but rather so that He could return glory!

You and I are meant to live lives of glory so we can in turn point to the one who gives the glory. This is the purpose of our renovation, so that it will lead to a transformed, transfigured, glorified life that is able to return glory back to our wonderful God.

With all that has been said about "kingdom come" theology (Matthew 6) and the knowledge of the glory of the Lord covering the earth like the waters cover the sea (Habakkuk 2:14), we fall into a subtle deception and reduce those truths to event-based versus life-based.

When we pray for His kingdom to come, we tend to hope for an event in which God will manifest His kingdom on the earth so the world will want to flock to that event, thinking that His kingdom has come. And while there is truth to that, it's only a partial truth; you and I are meant to be a kingdom encounter for the world.

> You are an encounter with the kingdom of heaven for the world. People are meant to discover what the glory of God looks like because they've had encounters with people who live in glory!

When Jesus sent His disciples out to minister, He told them that when they healed people, they should say that the kingdom of heaven had come near to them. What's the point of that? You are an encounter with the kingdom of heaven for the world. People are meant to discover what the glory of God looks like because they've had encounters with people who live in glory!

Living with an event-based perspective of the manifested kingdom of God is to irresponsibly sidestep our call as disciples to share the full gospel to the world.

So how do we live in this glorified way? Many have sought it through being prayed for by revival leaders. There's nothing wrong with that, but it isn't the way. Many go from conference to conference, hoping for a moment when God suddenly and miraculously changes everything. There's nothing wrong with that, either, but it isn't the way.

The way was made clear by Paul:

> *I appeal to you therefore, brothers, by the mercies of God, to present your bodies as a living sacrifice, holy and acceptable to God, which is*

your spiritual worship. Do not be conformed to this world, but be transformed by the renewal of your mind, *that by testing you may discern what is the will of God, what is good and acceptable and perfect.*

—Romans 12:1–2 (emphasis added)

In his book *Supernatural Power of a Transformed Mind,* Bill Johnson points out that the above verse is bridged to Jesus' transfiguration in Mark 9.[2]

And after six days Jesus took with him Peter and James and John, and led them up a high mountain by themselves. And he was transfigured before them, and his clothes became radiant, intensely white, as no one on earth could bleach them. And there appeared to them Elijah with Moses, and they were talking with Jesus.

—Mark 9:2–4

Johnson points out that the same word is used for both transformed and transfigured: *metamorphoo.*

...to transform (literally or figuratively, "metamorphose"):—change, transfigure, transform.[3]

That word is where we get the word metamorphosis, to change from one form to another. A good example would be a caterpillar changing into a butterfly. It's the same creature but a totally different form.

This divine brightness is the glory of the open heaven that we are meant to shine upon the world. And we play an important part in the full manifestation of that glory through a renovation of our minds.

---

2 Bill Johnson, *Supernatural Power of a Transformed Mind* (Shippensburg, PA: Destiny Image, 2013).

3 Olive Tree Enhanced Strong's Dictionary, computer software, version 2011, Olive Tree Bible Software, accessed November 2, 2016 (www.olivetree.com).

A Renovated Mind

An open heaven is engaged through the renovation of our minds. Let's look at Romans 12 one more time.

> *I appeal to you therefore, brothers, by the mercies of God, to present your bodies as a living sacrifice, holy and acceptable to God, which is your spiritual worship. Do not be conformed to this world, but be* trans-formed by the renewal of your mind, *that by testing you may discern what is the will of God, what is good and acceptable and perfect.*
> —Romans 12:1–2 (emphasis added)

The word renewal here literally means to renovate. In a renovation, you get a better version of the original. If I renovate my kitchen, I get a better kitchen. But in our case, if we renovate our minds, not only do we get a better mind, but we get a glorified life.

The renovation of your mind is not achieved through trying to think different thoughts.

Over the years, Christians have heard over and over again that they need to change the way they think. The problem is that I don't even know how I think. (I've certainly been asked *if* I think, but that's another story.)

We don't have to change how we think. We have to change where we think from.

Let me explain.

When a little child sees the beautiful red glow of a burner on the stove, they're instantly drawn to touch it. When they discover through the pain of being burnt that red means hot, they learn not to touch. From that point on, a learned thought process determines how that child relates to the stove.

In the same way, we may have a bad experience in a relationship and our learned response is mistrust toward other relationships. Or a bad business deal may lead to a learned response of fear to other business deals. There are a myriad of other examples I could give, but at the end of the day, past experiences end up dictating present behaviour.

Doesn't that sound like a lot of people? They're labelled and imprisoned by their past, and subsequently paralyzed in their present because of their past.

The renovation that has to take place, so we can walk in the glory that God has for us, is found in no longer thinking from the past but rather thinking from heaven. The renovation is to fully engage thinking the same way that heaven thinks about things.

> *But the* wisdom from above *is first pure, then peaceable, gentle, open to reason, full of mercy and good fruits, impartial and sincere. And a* harvest of righteousness *is sown in peace by those who make peace.*
> —James 3:17–18 (emphasis added)

For example, earthly wisdom would say that we need wealth; heaven operates from the perspective of abundance. What's the difference? Earthly wisdom says that wealth must be stewarded for it not to run out. So we save. Heaven's perspective is that there is no end to the supply. So we are generous. This is just one example of the differences between heavenly wisdom and earthly wisdom.

> *But if you have bitter jealousy and selfish ambition in your hearts, do not boast and be false to the truth. This is* not the wisdom that comes down from above, *but is earthly, unspiritual, demonic. For where jealousy and selfish ambition exist, there will be disorder and every vile practice.*
> —James 3:14–16 (emphasis added)

So how do we do this? How do we engage the way heaven thinks? It starts by understanding an important truth. Heaven thinks higher.

> *For my thoughts are not your thoughts, neither are your ways my ways, declares the Lord. For as the* heavens are higher than the earth, *so are* my ways higher than your ways *and* my thoughts than your thoughts.
> —Isaiah 55:8–9 (emphasis added)

Imagine a first grade student learning the first mathematical principles of addition and subtraction. Now, put that first grader into a college calculus class. From the first grader's view, the college formulas probably wouldn't even look like math. While both students are engaged in mathematics, the college student is operating at a higher level of understanding.

There is an understanding in the unseen realm of God that is above the earthly realm. And while it is above us, it is available to us if we pursue it.

However, we have a free will. We can choose if we want to embrace kingdom ways. We can choose to stay in the confines of our finite minds and close the door on the infinite.

Or we can renovate to engage the glory.

"Prove to Be My Disciples."

By this my Father is glorified, that you bear much fruit and so prove to be my disciples.

—John 15:8

This privileged lifestyle is for every disciple of Jesus, but I think we need to have a better definition of discipleship than the weak, selfish versions that seem to infect the body of Christ. In the next chapter, we will look at the privilege of being a disciple of Christ.

chapter two

The Two Levels
of Discipleship

IN HIS BOOK *THE FORGOTTEN WAYS*, ALAN HIRSCH ELOQUENTLY PRESENTS the importance of discipleship and its role in healthy Christian living. He says that the heart of it all, the bottom line, is that Jesus is Lord. I've heard Hirsch say it this way: "Jesus is Lord. Three words that are a worldview."

Three words that are a worldview. What an incredible statement! In other words, "Jesus is Lord" is the lens through which I view my life. Everything that relates to my life is viewed through the thought process of the lordship of Christ.

We are called to be disciples, not decisions, and while we rejoice with all of heaven when one sinner repents, that decision does not equate with discipleship. Sadly, many so-called Christians have made the decision that Jesus is Lord but have not integrated their decision *about* His lordship with a lifestyle that *reflects* His lordship. There is a vast difference between agreement with the statement about His lordship and submission to His lordship.

To agree with His lordship is to reflect His lordship.

> Sadly, many so-called Christians have made the decision that Jesus is Lord but have not integrated their decision *about* His lordship with a lifestyle that *reflects* His lordship.

Going Beyond the Doorway

*And someone said to him, "Lord, will those who are saved be few?"
And he said to them, "Strive to enter through the narrow door.
For many, I tell you, will seek to enter and will not be able. When once
the master of the house has risen and shut the door, and you begin to
stand outside and to knock at the door, saying, 'Lord, open to us,' then
he will answer you, 'I do not know where you come from.' Then you
will begin to say, 'We ate and drank in your presence, and you taught in
our streets.' But he will say, 'I tell you, I do not know where you come
from. Depart from me, all you workers of evil!' In that place there will
be weeping and gnashing of teeth, when you see Abraham and Isaac
and Jacob and all the prophets in the kingdom of God but you yourselves
cast out."*

—Luke 13:23–28 (emphasis added)

Those many who have made a decision about the lordship of Jesus, but
have not engaged the lifestyle of His lordship, risk being like these who
stood by the door but were left outside when the Master closed the door.

It is not enough to be at the door; we must enter through it. We
must engage in relationship with King Jesus, which leads to His kingdom
manifesting through our lives. What I'm trying to gently say is that Jesus
is expecting more from us than a decision.

What does this have to do with discipleship? Submission to His
lordship is where discipleship begins. The gate is our decision, but entering requires submission.

Over the years, I have laboured to define discipleship. I've landed
on two statements: "Discipleship is a lifestyle of deliberate submission
to the lordship of Jesus" and "Always seek permission instead of presuming to know what to do." Or said more succinctly, "permission, not
presumption."

Let's look at what these phrases mean.

Deliberate submission means making a conscious decision to submit to what He wants above what we want. It's simple and causes us to
live with an awareness of heaven's perspective of our lives. There is great

value to this, because being aware of heaven awakens our hearts to the goodness of God. That awakening leads us to intimacy, which protects us from religion and leads to holiness.

Holiness and religion look a lot alike, but it's important to note that they are vastly different. Like a counterfeit hundred dollar bill that looks like the real thing but holds no value, so too religion looks like holiness, but to the Lord it holds no value. Religion requires us to behave in certain ways to gain acceptance. It has *"the appearance of godliness, but [denies] its power"* (2 Timothy 3:5). Intimacy, however, causes us to gain more intimacy, drawing us closer to Him, which results in holiness. "Holy" is best defined as being set apart. A holy life is one that is set apart because of one's relationship with God.

The simplest way to live out deliberate submission is to ask before doing. It's a lifestyle of asking for His opinion, getting the go-ahead from our Lord before moving forward. Asking permission may seem childlike, but doing things without permission is childish. More on that shortly.

Seeking permission puts value on the thoughts of heaven and moves us from awareness to engagement. Through the process of asking for permission, we learn to hear God speak over the activities of our lives. There is great value in learning to hear the Lord speak. We want to be those sheep who know His voice (John 10:27). So often people want to hear the voice of God over the big things in their lives but can't hear Him because they don't practice hearing Him in the little things.

Seeking permission has one other exceptional protective quality: it protects us from doing what is good. Follow my reasoning. Let's look back to the beginning of time, to the tree whose fruit put mankind into bondage in the first place.

> *And out of the ground the Lord God made to spring up every tree that is pleasant to the sight and good for food. The tree of life was in the midst of the garden, and the tree of the* knowledge of good and evil.
> —Genesis 2:9 (emphasis added

There were two trees—the Tree of Life and the Tree of the Knowledge of Good and Evil. We've become really good at labelling the evil side of that tree. However, we should remember that it's the knowledge of *good* and evil.

It is possible to do good things that are not godly.

On that day many will say to me, "Lord, Lord, did we not prophesy in your name, and cast out demons in your name, and do many mighty works in your name?" And then will I declare to them, "I never knew you; depart from me, you workers of lawlessness."

—Matthew 7:22–23 (emphasis added)

The Greek wording for workers of lawlessness, *ergazomai anomia*, is like saying "working illegally." This is why seeking permission is such an important aspect of the disciple's life. Not all good work is going to bring life. People often busy themselves with good things but aren't truly engaged in *God* things.

Let's establish this: God is good. All things that are done in association with Him will be good and bring life. However, the enemy will set a snare for those who aren't at a place of submission to the Lord. These snares may include good things that take up one's energy, time, and resources and yet aren't in His will. These people work in an unauthorized fashion.

It's like the counterfeit we talked of earlier. These works may look good, but they don't hold the value of godly works. Adam and Eve thought it would be *good* to have the same information God had. Later they discovered that what they had *presumed* to be good wasn't good at all.

So is it possible to be ensnared by doing good? Yes, if it isn't asking or leading you to do it. But there's a simple way to protect yourself: do what the Lord has authorized. It's all about permission, not presumption. Ask, and learn His voice. He is a God who speaks to us. We just need to learn to hear Him.

The Apostle Paul lived this principle:

And they went through the region of Phrygia and Galatia, having been forbidden by the Holy Spirit to speak the word in Asia. And when they had come up to Mysia, they attempted to go into

Bithynia, but the Spirit of Jesus did not allow them. *So, passing by Mysia, they went down to Troas. And a vision appeared to Paul in the night: a man of Macedonia was standing there, urging him and saying,* "Come over to Macedonia and help us." *And when Paul had seen the vision, immediately we sought to go on into Macedonia,* concluding that God had called us to preach the gospel to them.

So, setting sail from Troas, we made a direct voyage to Samothrace, and the following day to Neapolis…

—Acts 16:6–11 (emphasis added)

Paul sought permission and didn't presume to know what was good. It seemed good to go to some places, but the Spirit of the Lord stopped him. Then, in a dream, the Lord gave Paul the assignment He wanted him to fulfill.

The gospel is good and it would have been good in Asia, but that wasn't what God wanted. It would have been good in Bithynia, too, but that wasn't what God wanted. What He *did* want was for them to go to Macedonia. So they went.

This form of clarity with the Spirit was modelled by the apostles after they held a council meeting to determine what to do about circumcising new believers.

For it has seemed good to the Holy Spirit and to us *to lay on you no greater burden than these requirements…*

—Acts 15:28 (emphasis added)

All of us, at one point or another, have had the experience of entering into something we presumed was good only to discover after a period of time that it wasn't good at all. We can avoid these situations by learning to walk in His permission.

So, in this posture of seeking permission, we develop a submitted lifestyle and at the same time gain intimacy and clarity in hearing His voice. That seems like a good exchange, but there's more.

Submit yourselves therefore to God. Resist the devil, and he will flee from you.

—James 4:7

James exposes us to a great truth. The greater the submission, the greater the authority we have over the enemy. What does the devil fleeing look like? To me, it looks like sickness and disease leaving our bodies, like torment leaving and poverty being broken… you know, the stuff Jesus said that His disciples would do.

And these signs will accompany those who believe: *in my name they will cast out demons; they will speak in new tongues; they will pick up serpents with their hands; and if they drink any deadly poison, it will not hurt them; they will lay their hands on the sick, and they will recover.*

—Mark 16:17–18 (emphasis added)

The absolutes of the kingdom of heaven cannot be released to anything other than a submitted heart. Why? Because the power of God is meant to manifest His agenda and the nature of His heart, not ours. The degree to which we surrender to God will be proportional to the measure of the manifestation of His power.

But in the pursuit of discovering the ancient pillars, I found another level of discipleship that's available to us.

Building from a Foundation

Delight yourself in the Lord, and he will give you the desires of your heart. Commit your way *to the Lord; trust in him, and he will act.*

—Psalm 37:4–5 (emphasis added)

These verses appear to contradict what I shared earlier about submitting our hearts. After all, submission means laying down what we want and picking up what God wants. It's saying, "Not my will, but Yours, be done." It's the process of picking up our crosses and following Him.

I used to justify this scripture and others like it by saying that I would lay down what I wanted and exchange those desires for God's desires. It was a sort of divine exchange. Sounds holy, doesn't it? Through the exchange, He would release His desires in me, and by default they would be my desires.

I was wrong.

Let's take a moment to look at King David's life and how this manifested for Him. In 1 Chronicles 17, David shares with Nathan his desire to build a house for the Lord. Nathan tells David to go for it because God is with him.

However, the Lord spoke to Nathan that night. For the sake of space, I'll paraphrase. God said that He had journeyed with Israel from tent to tent and never asked for a home of His own. He also said that it wasn't for David to build His house. A little later on, in 1 Chronicles 28, we learn the reason: David was a man of war.

But God goes on to say that David's desire would be fulfilled by one of his sons, Solomon. God also goes on to promise wonderful things over David's lineage and Israel. So great were God's promises over David and his family that David was overwhelmed by God's goodness.

God, in a desire to accomplish what was on David's heart, devised a plan that would satisfy His righteousness while accomplishing David's desire. In a sense, He said, "That's an amazing idea, David, but I'll even make it better!"

God wants to give us our desires. If it were not so, Jesus was mistaken when He said to His disciples,

> *Truly, truly, I say to you, whatever you ask of the Father in my name,*
> *he will give it to you. Until now you have asked nothing in my name.*
> *Ask, and you will receive, that your joy may be full.*
>
> —John 16:23–24

"Whatever you ask." That seems like a pretty big promise! What do we do with this?

17

Let's look at the first level of discipleship as being foundational. God will only bless someone's dream if they have a submitted heart. God is committed to the desires of a submitted heart. In other words, if you want God to commit to you, you need to submit to Him.

For the eyes of the Lord run to and fro throughout the whole earth, to give strong support to those whose heart is blameless toward him.

—2 Chronicles 16:9 (emphasis added)

As for the second level of discipleship, I believe a time is upon us when God will release His favour and blessing on His children like never before in history. I believe that the outpouring of His Spirit and kingdom are coming in such a way that when the world will look upon the Church, they'll earnestly desire the things they see manifesting in His Bride, both spiritually and naturally. The days of the Church being the scourge of society because of its apparent intolerance and hypocrisy are over. The Lord will cause His blessings to be released amongst His own in a way that will cause the world to echo the words of the Psalmist:

When the Lord restored the fortunes of Zion, we were like those who dream. Then our mouth was filled with laughter, and our tongue with shouts of joy; then they said among the nations, "The Lord has done great things for them." *The Lord has done great things for us; we are glad.*

—Psalm 126:1–3 (emphasis added)

The restoration of the Church's fortunes will cause joy to be seen in the world. Truly the world will cry, "The Lord has done great things for them!" The great things which the Lord has done for us will be like the light that draws nations from the darkness (Isaiah 60). They will see that light in their darkness—that favour, that kingdom—and run to the Saviour who will intercede on their behalf as He answers our prayers and fulfills our joy, all as a witness to the world, declaring the goodness of a great God!

The Two Levels of Discipleship

This is why engaging the first level of discipleship is so vital for the body of Christ. If we don't create a safe place for dreams by submitting our hearts, we cannot walk in the fullness of the blessing of God.

So let's examine the second level of discipleship—or, in other words, the manifestation of the kingdom of God—with the understanding that the first level acts as a foundation for these greater things.

Hope deferred makes the heart sick, but a desire fulfilled is a tree of life.
—Proverbs 13:12

Much is written and spoken of in the first half of the above verse. And we know that it's true: hope deferred does make our hearts sick. However, that's not the end of the verse—or the promise. The promise is that a desire fulfilled is a tree of life.

In Genesis, the angel was set at the gate of the Garden of Eden to protect Adam and Eve from eating of the Tree of Life. There was a danger of them living forever in their fallen state. There is an eternality about the Tree of Life. In other words, our fulfilled desires are meant to be a source of eternal blessing for us, and the world around us, on both sides of eternity.

Consider the condition of the world around you, including your friends, co-workers, and family who don't know the blessing of the Lord. Consider how often their hearts are sickened by the condition of the world they live in. In whatever way the enemy has robbed hope from them, God desires to make your life an example of His goodness. He desires for the fulfillment of your desires to be a source of eternal blessing for them. In a sense, the fulfilment of your desires are like a tree of life.

Now, let's look at the second manifestation of the kingdom.

And your ears shall hear a word behind you, saying, "This is the way, walk in it," when you turn to the right or when you turn to the left.
—Isaiah 30:21 (emphasis added)

And let's look again at Psalms 37:

Delight yourself in the Lord, and he will give you the desires of your heart. Commit your way *to the Lord; trust in him, and he will act.*

—Psalm 37:4–5 (emphasis added)

In both of these passages we see the same Hebrew word, *derek,* which means:

> ...*way, road, distance, journey, manner... road, way, path... journey... direction... manner, habit, way... of course of life... of moral character...*[4]

Often we think of the will of God as being directional only. That's like describing a flower by saying it has a stem. While you would be correct, there's more to the flower than just the stem. So, too, is the will of God about more than just direction. It is also conditional on how we do things.

In Isaiah 30:21, we see that the choice of going either to right or left is given to the hearer. The promise ("This is the way") is given afterward. That word, *derek,* while having directional connotations, also shows us how to do something. So we can also understand this passage to mean "This is how" or "This is the kingdom way."

We don't need to live in the worry of hitting or missing the will of God directionally if we're living the will of God conditionally. In fact, Isaiah 30:21 gives us the freedom to choose the direction we want to go. Then we are coached in the manner of how we should walk it out. That is part of our desires being fulfilled. Isn't that liberating?

Let me say it another way. You no longer have to fret over which direction you're supposed to go. Rather, you can look down each path and see whether you can fully engage the nature of the kingdom of heaven on that path. And if you're able to engage His kingdom on either path, you get to pick the one you like most.

God eventually wants you to be able to choose what you desire.

---

4 Olive Tree Enhanced Strong's Dictionary, computer software, version 2011, Olive Tree Bible Software, accessed November 2, 2016 (www.olivetree.com).

I am confident that Satan wouldn't want us engaging the ways of the kingdom. So if we can't see ourselves fully engaging the kingdom down a particular path, or if we're prohibited from it, why would we ever choose to go down that path? So much for being deceived!

So let's move forward from the concept of deliberate submission to seeing our desires fulfilled. Let's mature to walking in the ways of the kingdom.

One last thing. Let's say you've moved forward, but you're in a situation where you just can't seem to find your way. You're not sure of the kingdom way, or you're not sure if the desire you would like fulfilled comes from an area of the heart that you haven't submitted. Well, when you don't know what to do, do what you know. You can always go back to deliberate submission, or go back to seeking permission instead of presuming what to do. You always can return to your foundations to protect yourself from your own agenda getting in the way of God's.

At this point, you may be asking, "So how do I find out about the kingdom ways?" The kingdom ways, or the absolutes of God, are found in a renewed mind. The mind of Christ.

chapter three

Obtaining the Mind of Christ

Yet among the mature we do impart wisdom, although it is not a wisdom of this age or of the rulers of this age, who are doomed to pass away. But we impart a secret and hidden wisdom of God, which God decreed before the ages for our glory. None of the rulers of this age understood this, for if they had, they would not have crucified the Lord of glory. But, as it is written, "What no eye has seen, nor ear heard, nor the heart of man imagined, what God has prepared for those who love him."

—1 Corinthians 2:6–9

I HAVE OFTEN HEARD IT SAID THAT FAITH IS THE CURRENCY OF HEAVEN. I entirely disagree with that terrible theology. It allows for a works-based perspective of faith that brings Christians into the bondage of thinking that if they have enough faith, they can purchase a miracle from heaven.

Think of it this way. When I go to an ATM to access funds from my bank, I use a debit card. Let's say I want to withdraw twenty dollars. I use my card and get the money. Now let's say I want to get one hundred dollars. I don't use a bigger card; I use the same card to access the funds. In the same way, I don't have a bigger card for a thousand dollar withdrawal. I use the same card.

You don't use faith like a resource. It's your access to the resource. And if faith is like the debit card, then the renovated mind is like the ATM machine that accesses heaven's bank. How we think will determine whether or not we're able to access the resources of heaven.

We can see from 1 Corinthians 2:6 that the first step to obtaining the mind of Christ, which is the renovated mind, is to mature. Often Christians think that they've done enough by saying a prayer confessing their desire for Jesus to be their Saviour. While we don't doubt the doctrine of salvation, if there is no evidence of a transformed life, shouldn't the validity of the confession be brought into question?

Paul wrote, in the famous "love chapter":

When I was a child, I spoke like a child, I thought like a child, I reasoned like a child. When I became a man, I gave up childish ways.
—1 Corinthians 13:11

There is a great difference between childlike and childish. The mature believer has a childlike faith, a faith that trusts God at His word. Mature believers remain childlike, still able to be struck by wonder at the greatness of God. They have learned the power of prayer, the intimacy of worship, and the importance of obedience. The mature believer has gone deep enough to discover that there is much more to the Lord than the religious trap that deceives so many people. Maturity is being able to steward both the blessings of God and opportunities to grow in spirit by facing and defeating our adversary.

Sadly, though, there are far too many childish believers. They try to get God to do what they want by crying out or throwing temper tantrums. They walk in rebellion towards His lordship and focus on the cares of life on this side of eternity, having no concern for the thoughts of God on the other side. Spend a day in a home with children who are out of control, and I'm sure you'll understand the disappointment that the Father must feel over His childish disciples.

So how do we mature? Paul gives us a simple but clear instruction: give up your childish ways. It seems simple, but it can be difficult.

Here are three childish things to give up that will lead you to maturity. While these aren't exhaustive, if you address them you will move forward.

1. Your Truth, My Truth, Whose Truth?

The first childish things you must give up is the thought that truth should be relative.

Jesus said to him, "I am the way, and the truth, and the life. No one comes to the Father except through me."

—John 14:6

Truth is not relative. In our postmodern society, we've been forced to embrace the mindset that something might be good for you but it doesn't have to be good for me. While we must be careful not to create restrictive religious communities based on certain behaviours that determine the value and acceptance we receive, we do have a responsibility to individually embrace the truth that Jesus presents. A massive number of those who identify Jesus as Lord live in ways that don't reflect the truth He expects us to live out.

Truth is not relative. He has established truth. He has established what is right and wrong, and mature believers need to be interested only in His definitions. It's childish to say that something is okay for me so that I can get my way.

2. I Want My Way

The second childish thing that must be put aside is the desire to get your own way. Your way can't be engaged until you have totally submitted to His way. To mature, a believer must be willing to lay down his life and be *"crucified with Christ"* (Galatians 2:20). The burning faith questions of immature believers revolve around whether to sin or not sin. Or, for that matter, trying to determine what is or isn't sin.

This childishness affirms the relativism of truth. If we're not willing to lay down what we want, we'll twist the way we view truth to *get* our way. This immature form of discipleship puts us on the wrong side of spiritual warfare.

For though we walk in the flesh, we are not waging war according to the flesh. For the weapons of our warfare are not of the flesh but have divine power to destroy strongholds. We destroy arguments and every lofty opinion raised against the knowledge of God, and take every thought captive to obey Christ, being ready to punish every disobedience, when your obedience is complete.

—2 Corinthians 10:3–6

Rather than taking captive thoughts that exalt themselves above the knowledge of God, the immature believer promotes those thoughts to the throne room. Those thoughts lead to temptation and disobedience rather than godliness.

The fear of religion has led some to be religiously nonreligious. Instead of being in bondage to the religious spirit that promotes performance-based behaviour above a changed heart, there are those who are in bondage to a religious spirit that encourages behaviour that leads to compromise. Both bring the same result: a form of godliness with no power.

It is childish to think you should have your way while being unwilling to discover His way.

3. It's Not My Fault

The third childish thing that needs to be addressed is the issue of responsibility.

Therefore, my beloved, as you have always obeyed, so now, not only as in my presence but much more in my absence, work out your own salvation with fear and trembling, for it is God who works in you, both to will and to work for his good pleasure.

—Philippians 2:12–13

Paul admonishes individual believers in the church at Philippi to work out their own salvation with fear and trembling. You see, *you* are responsible for your salvation. You will stand before the Lord, alone, and give an account for the way you lived out the faith that you profess.

So why did he say *"with fear and trembling"*? Glad you asked.

Remember the whole relative truth thing we just chatted about? Here's an example of how it works. God, through scripture, defines forgiveness and how we are supposed to act upon it. He then says, "You go ahead and live your life any way you want, and My desire is that you would live this out My way. Because in the end, when I scrutinize your life, My definition will be *the* definition. No one else's."

You might reply, "Well, Your definition doesn't work for me." (By the way, if you do say that, tell me beforehand so I can be on the other side of heaven.) I'm pretty confident that when we see the Lord in all His glory, His way will seem pretty reasonable.

You're responsible for how you define godliness. You. No one else. You will not be able to blame or hide behind anyone. Each of us will give an account for the stewardship of our lives and His truth. Even as I write this, I tremble.

You may be saying to yourself, *I don't even know His definitions or His ways.* Let's look at 2 Peter. This passage is a little lengthy, but read it twice. It'll be worth it.

His divine power has granted to us all things that pertain to life and godliness, *through the knowledge of him who called us to his own glory and excellence, by which he has granted to* us his precious and very great promises, *so that through them you may become partakers of the divine nature, having escaped from the corruption that is in the world because of sinful desire. For this very reason, make every effort to supplement your faith with virtue, and virtue with knowledge, and knowledge with self-control, and self-control with steadfastness, and steadfastness with godliness, and godliness with brotherly affection, and brotherly affection with love. For if these qualities are yours and are increasing, they keep you from being ineffective or unfruitful in the knowledge of our Lord Jesus Christ. For whoever lacks these qualities is so nearsighted that he is blind, having forgotten that he was cleansed from his former sins. Therefore, brothers, be all the more diligent to confirm your calling and election, for if you practice these qualities you will never fall. For in this way there will be richly provided for you an entrance into the eternal kingdom of our Lord and Savior Jesus Christ.*

—2 Peter 1:3–11 (emphasis added)

The main point I want you to see from these verses is that it's all there. Everything you need to know about God's character—including His ways and His definitions—can be found in Scripture. You need to be in your Bible, and more than just a chapter a day to keep the devil away. He will reveal Himself to you through His word.

It's childish to think that you aren't responsible.

Let's continue to look at 1 Corinthians 2:

…these things God has revealed to us through the Spirit. For the Spirit searches everything, even the depths of God. For who knows a person's thoughts except the spirit of that person, which is in him? So also no one comprehends the thoughts of God except the Spirit of God. Now we have received not the spirit of the world, but the Spirit who is from God, that we might understand the things freely given us by God. And we impart this in words not taught by human wisdom but taught by the Spirit, interpreting spiritual truths to those who are spiritual.

—1 Corinthians 2:10–13 (emphasis added)

We live in an amazing age where information about virtually anything can be found with the click of a mouse or tap of a finger. And while I'm not a child of black-and-white television— or, like my dad would say, "We watched our shows on the radio"—I do remember a time when research meant going to a library and searching through indexes and scanning through tables of contents to find the information I needed. Now, various internet search engines can find hundreds if not thousands of potential sources of information for me. They boast that the information is found in less than a second. It's truly amazing if you grew up prior to the information age.

In 1 Corinthians 2:10–13, Paul shows us God's search engine: His Holy Spirit. Paul tells us that the Spirit searches everything, even the very depths of God. Take a moment and consider the possibilities of searching the depths of God. He is infinite. His depths don't stop... ever. This is the great value of our Helper, the Holy Spirit

> *These things I have spoken to you while I am still with you.* But the Helper, the Holy Spirit, whom the Father will send in my name, he will teach you all things and bring to your remembrance *all that I have said to you.*
>
> —John 14:25–26 (emphasis added)

We need the Holy Spirit to show us the deep things of God because only the infinite can search the infinite. This is why we cannot understand the ways of God without the Spirit in us. We cannot understand the infinite without guidance from the infinite. Paul was saying that we didn't receive the spirit of the creation, but of the Creator. Creation boasts of the glory of God, but it cannot explain it.

> We need the Holy Spirit to show us the deep things of God because only the infinite can search the infinite.

Through Christ, all that we need pertaining to life and godliness is freely available to us through the revelation of His ways by the Holy Spirit. However, the Spirit imparts spiritual wisdom, and Paul shows us that it only comes to those who are spiritual. What does that mean?

> *The natural person does not accept the things of the Spirit of God, for they are folly to him, and he is not able to understand them because they are spiritually discerned. The spiritual person judges all things, but is himself to be judged by no one. "For who has understood the mind of the Lord so as to instruct him?" But we have the mind of Christ.*
>
> —1 Corinthians 2:14–16

We must assume a particular posture to walk in the absolutes of God. The power of a renewed mind is released to those who have learned to embrace a spirit-led lifestyle.

Imagine having a conversation with someone while they're in your basement and you're on the roof. Is it possible to have a face-to-face conversation with them? Obviously not. As ridiculous as that would seem, many Christians live their lives trying to connect with God without understanding that they're on different floors!

God is spirit, and those who worship him must worship in spirit and truth.
—John 4:24

This scripture is packed with a vital truth for those who wish to understand the ways of God through His Spirit: you have to know what floor you're on. This understanding comes through knowing how we're made up.

Now may the God of peace himself sanctify you completely, and may your whole spirit and soul and body be kept blameless at the coming of our Lord Jesus Christ.
—1 Thessalonians 5:23

We see here that we are three parts: spirit, soul, and body.

Our body is easy to define. That is our fleshly man, our physical bodies.

Our spirit is the part of us that connects with God. It is made up of the deep stuff, the gateway to being conformed into His image. Our deep is called to by His deep.

Deep calls to deep at the roar of your waterfalls; all your breakers and your waves have gone over me.
—Psalm 42:7

The spirit is the part of us that can contain "God stuff," because our spirit is made to have fellowship with God.

Our soul is our mind, will, and emotions. It is where we think, feel, and choose. This is the realm of authority in our lives. How we think or feel will determine what we choose to do. In a sense, the soul is the governing seat of us as human beings.

My point is, if you're trying to connect with God from the soul or the body, you're going to be frustrated. Because He is found on the spirit floor.

That which is born of the flesh is flesh, and that which is born of the Spirit is spirit.

—John 3:6

The Checks and Balances of Governing

Our great God is such a romantic. He would rather risk being rejected than force love.

In His desire to be chosen, He created us in such a fashion as to have a set of checks and balances in our framework so as to protect us from being forced into discipleship. He doesn't want robots; He wants lovers.

Here is the governmental definition of checks and balances:

Governmental: Extension of the separation of powers doctrine, under which each branch of a government can (if necessary) counter the actions or decisions of the other branches. This arrangement ensures transparency, and prevents domination of the government by any branch.[5]

In government, it's called checks and balances. In the believer, it's called free will.

Let's imagine a government that we'll call Christian. This is a democratic government, so Christian relies on a majority of votes to pass any motions. Let's say there are three parties in this ten-seat government; they are Spirit, Soul, and Body. The Spirit Party has won four seats, the Body Party has won three seats, and the Soul Party has won three seats as well.

The Spirit Party has won what is called a minority government; while they're the party with the most seats, they do not have enough votes

---

5 *Business Dictionary*, "Check and Balances." Date of access: October 4, 2016 (http://www.businessdictionary.com/definition/checks-and-balances.html#ixzz28BtMKmxf).

to garner a majority, which would allow them to make decisions on their own. Governing will be interesting, because to pass any motions, the Spirit Party will need to get one of the other parties to agree to the motion.

Let's be clear: the Spirit Party and the Body Party are polar opposites. All of their policies are in direct conflict with each other. There's no chance that the members of the Body Party will ever choose to agree with the Spirit Party (see Galatians 5:16–17). The Soul Party, however, can be influenced. They really don't have a strong platform of values, so they find themselves in the enviable position of having the real authority in this government.

For each motion, the Spirit Party will have to convince the Soul Party that their motion is good for Christian. Conversely, the Body Party will also lobby the Soul Party to get its own majority vote.

To be spirit-led, we need to be convinced—in how we think, feel, and choose—that the way of the spirit is better than the way of the flesh. However, many Christians, because they haven't allowed their mind/soul to be renovated, allow the body (flesh) to have its way, which distances them from intimacy with God.

A minority government can govern by forming what's called a coalition, where one party agrees with the platform of another party. Indeed, Christian has two options; it can become either spiritual or natural.

Let's look back at the verses from 1 Corinthians 2.

> The natural person does not accept the things of the Spirit of God, for they are folly to him, and he is not able to understand them because they are spiritually discerned. *The spiritual person judges all things, but is himself to be judged by no one. "For who has understood the mind of the Lord so as to instruct him?" But we have the mind of Christ.*
>
> —1 Corinthians 2:14–16 (emphasis added)

The natural person, whose majority vote has been established between a partnership between the soul and flesh, won't accept the things of the spirit. Why? Because those things don't make natural sense. Oh, this person may have heard of supernatural ways, but that's foolishness. They say things like, "Yes, we're supposed to have faith, but within reason" or "Yes, be giving, but be careful with the whole God-owns-it-all thing."

We know there is a natural way of doing things, but we also know there is a supernatural way, and the supernatural way is much better. The way to engage the supernatural ways of God is to create a coalition between the spirit and soul.

For the soul to fully embrace the platform of the spirit, the soul has to be renovated.

I'm from Canada. Many people come from other nations to live and work here. The majority of people in my province, Alberta, speak English. Let's imagine that a young man comes from Germany to work in Alberta. He arrives but doesn't speak any English. Over the course of a few months, he learns a few phrases to help him communicate. Over time, he grows in his understanding and becomes reasonably fluent.

Now, he goes through an interesting transition. He understands and speaks English, but he's still translating his thoughts from German. He hears a phrase, translates it in his head to German, devises his response in German, and then translates it to English before replying. What's going on in his mind is still foreign to the country he's living in.

However, after some more time, he begins to understand and speak without having to translate in his mind. In fact, he finds himself thinking in English rather than German. He may even have a hard time remembering how to speak German. His integration into his new culture is complete, because he no longer thinks in the language of his old country.

Renovating our minds means making a shift from thinking like we did as natural people to thinking as heaven thinks.

So what do we do? Keep on sinning so God can keep on forgiving? I should hope not! If we've left the country where sin is sovereign, how can we still live in our old house there? Or didn't you realize we packed up and left there for good? That is what happened in baptism. When we went under the water, we left the old country of sin behind; when we came up out of the water, we entered into the new country of grace—a new life in a new land!

—Romans 6:1–3, The Message

What coalition exists in your life? Has the flesh managed to make a coalition with your soul, leading you into the natural man's way of thinking? Or have you created a coalition with the spirit and the ways of the Spirit of God?

The Pathway to the Renovated Mind

Let's return to our metaphor about the government of Christian. As with all governments, there are many motions to vote on. Every day, the Spirit Party and Body Party are lobbying the Soul Party to create a coalition for a majority vote.

It is in this foundational time of our discipleship that we learn to discern between the lobbying voices of the body and the spirit. It is when we learn deliberate submission to the lordship of Jesus and follow His leading. This happens in the early stages of our journey as we develop a heavenly mindset on life and prepare ourselves to walk in the "desires fulfilled" level of discipleship.

> *If then you have been raised with Christ, seek the things that are above, where Christ is, seated at the right hand of God.* Set your minds on things that are above, *not on things that are on earth. For you have died, and your life is hidden with Christ in God. When Christ who is your life appears, then you also will appear with him in glory.*
>
> —Colossians 3:1–4 (emphasis added)

Learning how to make a decision before you need to make a decision is the key to having a submitted heart.

Let's look at it a different way. I'm writing this chapter during the baseball playoffs. Baseball is a game of decisions.

So here's a scenario. It's the top of the ninth inning, there's a runner on first base, and there is one out. Where is the next play going to happen? For those of you who don't understand baseball, my apologies. But for those of who do, you know that the play is at second base. The runner at first has to run to second if the ball is hit, so there's a "force out"

33

at second. This opens up the option for a double play, which would end the inning.

Every player on the field knows that if the ball is hit to them, they're going to throw to second base to get the runner out. The third baseman knows, the second baseman knows, the centre fielder knows. Everyone is on the same page. Before the play happens, every player has decided what to do.

Therefore, the play will be a response, not a reaction.

Reaction is done under the influence of stimulus. When you react to temptation, whether through words or actions, you give authority to the stimulus. Reaction has only one imperative: "How do I get the best for me out of this?" This imperative is best defined in Scripture as the passions of the flesh (see Galatians 5:24, Ephesians 2:3).

A reaction is a decision made under duress. A response is a decision made out of conviction.

Christians who live by reacting make a daily coalition with the Body Party, or the passions of the flesh, in many of their decisions. Under the duress of temptation, pain, or pressure, the Body Party will look to take care of its passion, which is what feels best for itself.

Having many options can be stressful. The more options we entertain, the more our conviction diminishes.

We think that the more options we have, the better off we are. We think that having many pathways gives us power and importance. However, in the midst of weighing options, we have to consider the good and bad potential of each—and gamble that the good will outweigh the bad in our choices.

We think, *This is best for me. It will only hurt someone else a little.* Or, *I'm not getting what I need from this relationship. Even though it means splitting up the family, I have to take care of me right now.* We don't have permission to hurt others to make sure our needs are met first.

Response only has one option: the direction that was decided before the issue ever arrived.

34

Setting our minds on the things that are above has astounding potential for our lives. It means determining what we do *before* temptation comes. It is a predetermined decision.

We know how heaven responds to any issue. Remember 2 Peter 1:3? We have already been given all things pertaining to life and godliness, having decided before the issue arrives to respond the same way heaven does.

Here's one more way of defining a renewed mind. Below, I have drawn a cross with you at the intersection of the horizontal and vertical beams. The horizontal beam is "natural" and the vertical beam is "spiritual." The natural beam of the cross is shorter than the vertical beam; temporary things don't address the needs of our hearts like eternal things.

Now, imagine the picture as a compass. Compasses respond to the magnetic pull of true north. Earlier we looked at 1 Corinthians 2, where Paul identified the natural man versus the spiritual man. The pull of the natural man is to the natural beam (the temporary realm) and the pull of the spiritual man is to the spiritual beam (the King and His kingdom).

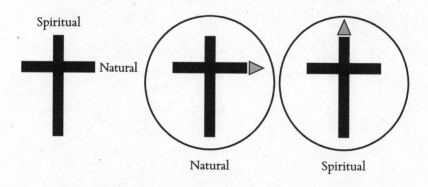

Simply stated, at the intersection of the cross, you have a choice to determine your true north. Which direction is your compass pointing?

Compartmentalization: The Enemy of Submission and Renewal

Every country has existing laws, motions that were passed by majority vote. The government of Christian, in our metaphor, also has previous laws due to past coalitions between the Soul Party with either the Body Party or the Spirit Party. These previous laws may prohibit Christian from walking in submission to the lordship of Jesus by creating compartmentalization, areas in which a decision has been made that the ways of heaven aren't applicable.

For example, at times people have come to me and said, "Pastor, I sure am blessed when you preach about the love of God, but when you talk about God being Lord over my time, well, I just don't agree with that." Or someone will tell me, "I love how God moves in the church, but you have to remember that my business is mine and I'll run it the way I see fit." I hear statements like that over and over again, with people saying that they agree with one aspect of the kingdom and apply it, but they disagree with another aspect.

This is called compartmentalization, and it's the archenemy of submission. Compartmentalization allows for Jesus to be Lord of certain areas of a person's life, but not others. Areas like salvation and grace? Sure! But areas like submission and forgiveness? Well, not so much.

Jesus spoke about the nature of His kingdom and addressed this issue through a parable:

> *He told them another parable.* "The kingdom of heaven is like leaven *that a woman took and hid in three measures of flour,* till it was all leavened.*"
>
> —Matthew 13:33 (emphasis added)

What was He saying? He was saying that the kingdom is like yeast. If you put yeast in a lump of dough, it will cause the whole lump to rise. The kingdom of heaven can permeate every aspect of our lives, unless we forbid it by creating a compartment where Jesus isn't Lord.

His kingdom won't tolerate other gods before Him. The kingdom can and must affect all aspects of our lives. To live compartmentalized is to live fractured, or crippled. Compartmentalization greatly diminishes your potential, because it means God can't trust you.

Most would say that they want the abundance of heaven to be released in their lives financially. We know that God expects us to be good stewards of finances before the abundance will come. But if you don't agree with His ways of stewardship, how can He trust you with His blessing of abundance? How can He release kingdom provision to those who don't agree with kingdom protocol?

When you submit your heart, you create an atmosphere of mutual trust between you and God. This trust is foundational in God's willingness to release the favour of heaven over us and over our dreams.

The second level of discipleship we talked about earlier is rooted in this trust. God wants to release you into your dreams. He wants to strongly support those who have turned their hearts towards Him. He desires to see your prayers answered and for your joy to be full! But He won't give that favour to anyone who doesn't have a submitted heart.

Why? Because God's power is so magnificent, and His favour so profound, that it will take you to places that can destroy you if your heart isn't totally His. Abundance can be a curse to those whose hearts can be compromised.

Let me put it another way. Imagine that you have two plastic bags. One has had holes punched in a line about an inch from the top; the other has not had holes punched in it. Now, fill each bag with water. The bag without holes can be filled to the very top, engaging the entire potential of the bag. The other can only be filled partially, because the holes will cause the bag to leak; its full potential can't be realized because the bag has been compromised.

God will only be able to pour His goodness and blessings up to our level of compromise. We complain because we feel like He isn't filling us up, but really it's the condition of our compromised, compartmentalized hearts that prohibit us from being filled.

Next, let's look at how we can renovate our minds.

chapter four

Let's Renovate!

So, HOW DO WE RENOVATE? HOW DO WE MOVE FROM THE NATURAL TO THE spiritual? How do we set our minds on the things that are above?

Much has been written and spoken about this subject. I would like to simplify it into three stages. These aren't steps that, when accomplished, turn eager fraternity pledges into members. No, these stages are built upon, and solidify intimacy with, Jesus.

At the end of it all, no matter how impressive any of our ministry or life endeavours are, they're meaningless without intimacy with Jesus.

Stage One: Confronting the Lies

For the weapons of our warfare are not of the flesh but have divine power to destroy strongholds. *We destroy* arguments and every lofty opinion *raised against the knowledge of God, and* take every thought captive *to obey Christ...*
            —2 Corinthians 10:4–5 (emphasis added)

It stands to reason that the enemy, because he lacks creative capacity, would use the very thing that God wants for us to engage—our minds—and pervert renewal into bondage. Paul writes that our weapons have divine power to destroy strongholds. He then goes on to define strongholds as arguments and lofty opinions. He wraps them all up as thoughts that need to be taken captive.

It stands to reason that the enemy, because he lacks creative capacity, would use the very thing that God wants for us to engage—our minds—and pervert renewal into bondage.

Here's how it works. The enemy operates in a perverse form of the renewal of the mind. Through various ways, he establishes a thought pattern based in a lie he has worked hard to build into our belief system. These are called strongholds, lie-based thought patterns.

How is the lie established? It can be any number of things—wounds, unforgiveness, offense, our own rebellion, sin, disappointment, unbelief, sickness, rejection... the list can go on. The issue is how we respond to these attacks.

Do two walk together, unless they have agreed to meet?

—Amos 3:3

Let me give you an example. Often strongholds are established when we're young, and kids can be influenced to be so mean. A little girl can be called ugly on the playground: "You're ugly. You look like a pig." The other kids laugh and make pig noises. It hurts her, but she stays brave and tries not to cry. Satan is viciously committed to his process of establishing a stronghold of thought, and he does everything he can to continue to affirm the lie he has sown. Over and over again, the girl hears that she is ugly. Her resolve slowly breaks down until one day she stands in front of a mirror and says, "You know what? They're right. I am ugly."

An agreement is entered into.

A stronghold is established.

A thought pattern is engaged.

And a lie is lived as truth.

As long as a lie is believed, it is the truth. This little girl will never believe that she is beautiful... as long as the lie is the truth. That is a stronghold.

The first stage to engaging a renewed mind is confronting lie-based thought patterns that contradict heaven's perspective.

I said before that this is not a step but a stage, and here's why. The lies have to be exposed. You can't expect someone who's caught in a maze to just decide not to be caught. You can't expect someone who's living what they believe to be the truth to just change. Someone has to come along, lift the covers, and reveal the truth that there are no monsters under the bed. The lie gets exposed in the context of intimacy with Jesus, where we are safe and truth can be revealed.

Search me, O God, and know my heart! Try me and know my thoughts! And see if there be any grievous way in me, and lead me in the way everlasting!

—Psalm 139:23–24

This stage is where we invite the Holy Spirit to search us and show us if we are living out any lies. Like I said, it's not a matter of changing how we think but changing where we think from.

I encourage you to take a moment to get quiet before the Lord. For me, it's a quiet place with worship music on. Ask Him to search your heart. Ask Him to show you strongholds. Pray the portion of the psalm above and listen. He wants to give you His kingdom.

Fear not, little flock, for it is your Father's good pleasure to give you the kingdom.

—Luke 12:32

When you've been able to quiet yourself, I invite you to pray:

Father, I thank You that You love me and I invite You by Your Holy Spirit to search my heart and reveal to me areas where I have believed lies. Show me where I have been deceived.

How can we be sure that what's revealed is a stronghold? Let's move to the next stage.

Stage Two: Accepting the Character

All demonic strongholds are based on Satan's first attack on mankind.

> *Now the serpent was more crafty than any other beast of the field that the Lord God had made.*
>
> *He said to the woman,* "Did God actually say, *'You shall not eat of any tree in the garden'?" And the woman said to the serpent, "We may eat of the fruit of the trees in the garden, but God said, 'You shall not eat of the fruit of the tree that is in the midst of the garden, neither shall you touch it, lest you die.'" But the serpent said to the woman,* "You will not surely die. For God knows that when you eat of it your eyes will be opened, and you will be like God, knowing good and evil."
>
> —Genesis 3:1–5 (emphasis added)

The root of all strongholds is found here in Genesis 3. In one way or another, the devil wants us to question the character of God. Will God provide? Will God love? Does God comfort? Let's look at what His character is like:

> *Long ago, at many times and in many ways, God spoke to our fathers by the prophets, but in these last days he has spoken to us by his Son, whom he appointed the heir of all things, through whom also he created the world.* He is the radiance of the glory of God and the exact imprint of his nature, *and he upholds the universe by the word of his power. After making purification for sins, he sat down at the right hand of the Majesty on high, having become as much superior to angels as the name he has inherited is more excellent than theirs.*
>
> —Hebrews 1:1–4 (emphasis added)

> *In their case the god of this world has blinded the minds of the unbelievers, to keep them from seeing the light of the gospel of the glory of Christ,* who is the image of God.
>
> —2 Corinthians 4:4 (emphasis added)

Here's the point. Do you want to know what God, your Heavenly Father, is like? Take a look at Jesus. He is the exact imprint of the nature of God. How Jesus acted, loved, reacted, cared, healed, spoke, encouraged, blessed, and so on, is exactly how the Father does the same. Jesus agreed with this:

> *Jesus said to him, "I am the way, and the truth, and the life. No one comes to the Father except through me.* If you had known me, you would have known my Father also. *From now on you do know him and have seen him."*
>
> *Philip said to him, "Lord, show us the Father, and it is enough for us."*
>
> *Jesus said to him, "Have I been with you so long, and you still do not know me, Philip?* Whoever has seen me has seen the Father. *How can you say, 'Show us the Father'? Do you not believe that* I am in the Father and the Father is in me? *The words that I say to you I do not speak on my own authority, but the Father who dwells in me does his works. Believe me that* I am in the Father and the Father is in me, or else believe on account of the works themselves."
>
> —John 14:6–11 (emphasis added)

I don't need to restate what Jesus was saying about Himself and the Father being one—He made it pretty clear—but I want to highlight one thing: *"believe on account of the works themselves."* He was saying, "If seeing Me hasn't been enough to show you that I'm like My Father, then look at what I've done. Look at how I've lived and let that be confirmation to you."

In this stage of accepting His character, we allow ourselves to be convinced that He is who He says He is. We are renovating our thinking.

Stage Three: Engaging the Truth

We come at last to the final stage in breaking a stronghold and completing the renovation: engaging truth.

Let's Renovate!

Earlier I quoted Amos 3:3 and shared how the establishment of a stronghold occurs when we agree with the lie and embrace it as truth. Having confronted Satan's lies and accepted the character of God, we can now move forward and break the agreement.

I have good news for you: nothing has been written in the cold stone bricks of a stronghold that cannot be erased by the Blood of Jesus.

> *And you, who were dead in your trespasses and the uncircumcision of your flesh, God made alive together with him, having forgiven us all our trespasses, by canceling the* record of debt that stood against us with its legal demands. *This he set aside, nailing it to the cross. He disarmed the rulers and authorities and put them to open shame, by triumphing over them in him.*
>
> —Colossians 2:13–15 (emphasis added)

Satan's Last Stand

When the enemy sees that he's losing the battle and risks the destruction of his stronghold, he throws out some outlandish lies in desperation. Here's the first lie: "You're a bad person. You should be rejected. You don't deserve forgiveness because you chose to agree with a lie." As usual, he provides enough fact to confuse it with truth. Yes, you did make that choice, but under deception. No fish knowingly bites a hook; the fish thinks it's food, not a trap. God won't hold sin against us if we're willing to embrace His Son.

> *…that is, in Christ God was reconciling the world to himself,* not counting their trespasses against them, *and entrusting to us the message of reconciliation.*
>
> —2 Corinthians 5:19 (emphasis added)

The second lie is even more ridiculous: "I am too strong. You can never be free from this. You are my prisoner." Here's a truth we can use to combat this lie. Jesus made this comment while addressing the nature of the kingdom of darkness:

When a strong man, fully armed, guards his own palace, his goods are safe; but when one stronger than he attacks him and overcomes him, he takes away his armor in which he trusted and divides his spoil.
—Luke 11:21–22 (emphasis added)

The strong man (Satan) is fully armed through a stronghold, and his treasures (his prisoners) are secure. But when the One who is stronger comes and attacks him, He destroys the armour that the strong man depended on and takes back the treasures.

The lie that deceived you may be strong, the devil and his ways may be strong, but I have great news for you: Jesus is stronger!

Engage that truth and see how strong Jesus really is.

The Process of Engaging Truth

To question and live contrary to the character of God is to sin. To live in a stronghold is to sin, so we confess it as sin and receive forgiveness for it.

If we confess our sins, he is faithful and just to forgive us our sins and to cleanse us from all unrighteousness.
—1 John 1:9

"But wait a minute," you say. "How is it sin if I was lied to? I didn't know I was sinning. That's not fair."

Let me explain. The sin isn't that you believed the lie; the sin is *agreeing* with the lie. We are being forgiven for agreeing with a lie that questions His character. Perhaps, in the midst of the stronghold, you sinned. Perhaps you believed a lie that led you to sin in other ways. Confess those as well and be forgiven.

Once we have confessed it as sin, we can break the agreement by repenting. I'll write more about the inner workings of repentance later, but for now let's move forward with the understanding that repentance is the rescinding of a former decision. Turning away, if you will.

Turning *from* something means we need to turn *to* something. That's what it means to engage the truth.

Since asking your Father to reveal strongholds, perhaps you've become aware of one that has held you in bondage. Once you've gotten clarity on what you need to accept regarding God's character, you can pray the prayer below.

Father, I see the stronghold that has kept me in bondage. I confess that I agreed with the lie I was told about Your character and I ask forgiveness. I also ask forgiveness for the sins I committed while under this bondage, and I'm sorry. Please forgive me, in Jesus' name. I thank You for Your faithfulness to Your Word, that if I confess my sin You will forgive me and cleanse me. I receive my forgiveness, in Jesus' name.

I now choose to repent and turn my back on the lie that was sown. I break and cancel my agreement with the enemy, and I also cancel every demonic assignment towards me on account of this broken stronghold. In Jesus' name, I command that this stronghold be totally destroyed. I command every demonic attachment to it to go directly to the feet of Jesus. Lord Jesus, I invite You to bring Your judgement on the enemy.

Father, I am free from this stronghold, and I now choose to engage the truth of Your character. I believe that You are good and I receive the fullness of Your wonderful nature in this area. You are good and Your love endures forever. Thank You for separating me from my sin and destroying this stronghold. I choose to be renewed in my mind in this area. In Jesus' name, amen.

It's good to be free.

Having an understanding of the renewal of the mind is foundational for these ancient pillars that hold up an open heaven. As I was to discover, however, these pillars are not doctrines but rather mindsets, non-negotiable perspectives, defining decisions about Him and us. They are pillars of a renewed mind.

But before I could tackle the pillars, I needed a starting place. That led to digging into the nature of His kingdom and healthy postures we should take within it.

chapter five

The Ever-Increasing Kingdom

For to us a child is born, to us a son is given; and the government shall
be upon his shoulder, and his name shall be called Wonderful Counselor,
Mighty God, Everlasting Father, Prince of Peace. Of the increase of
his government and of peace there will be no end, *on the throne*
of David and over his kingdom, to establish it and to uphold it with
justice and with righteousness from this time forth and forevermore. The
zeal of the Lord of hosts will do this.

—Isaiah 9:6–7 (emphasis added)

THE KINGDOM OF HEAVEN, CONTINUES TO INCREASE. HAVING THE RELATIONSHIP
of a disciple with Jesus is a relationship of growth and gain. We must
never stop growing. As we increase our capacity to understand His great
kingdom, we increase our potential to contain more of it. And there is always more of the kingdom of God. It is a kingdom that never ends. Our
lives need to reflect that truth. On this side of eternity, we never arrive
at a level of belief that makes us "complete" in our revelation of God.

The reason His kingdom continually increases is that He is infinite.
He has no end. Consider the scene in heaven right now.

…and before the throne there was as it were a sea of glass, like crystal.
And around the throne, on each side of the throne, are four living
creatures, full of eyes in front and behind: the first living creature like a

lion, the second living creature like an ox, the third living creature with the face of a man, and the fourth living creature like an eagle in flight. And the four living creatures, each of them with six wings, are full of eyes all around and within, and day and night they never cease to say, "Holy, holy, holy, is the Lord God Almighty, who was and is and is to come!"

—Revelation 4:6–8

> This is our Heavenly Father God—ever-increasing, never stagnant, and full of wonder. Our relationship with Him is meant to be the same.

Imagine these great creatures, full of eyes, taking in the majesty of God Himself. Each time they look at our great God, His ever-increasing ways allow them to see a new revelation of His goodness, causing them to explode with glorious praise and worship in wonder of Him.

This is our Heavenly Father God—ever-increasing, never stagnant, and full of wonder. Our relationship with Him is meant to be the same.

Forward or Backward

An increasingly dangerous lie has crept into our thinking. We've been deceived into believing that spiritual stagnancy is rest. In other words, we believe that we can achieve a level of spirituality and then remain there without maintaining it or challenging it to grow. And we're defining it as rest. Our human bodies are a testimony against that lie. Without exercise our bodies weaken, no matter what level of health we may have achieved.

In our spiritual walk, if we don't continue to move forward, dullness of hearing will cause us to regress spiritually. This is an important truth: you will either be going forward or backward.

To remain in the elementary is to regress. Do not mistake this statement as devaluing or dismissing the elementary principles; rather it puts them in their proper place of importance.

About this we have much to say, and it is hard to explain, since you have become dull of hearing. *For though* by this time you ought to be teachers, *you need someone to* teach you again the basic principles of the oracles of God. You need milk, not solid food, *for everyone* who lives on milk is unskilled in the word of righteousness, since he is a child. But solid food is for the mature, *for those who have their powers of discernment trained by constant practice to distinguish good from evil.*

—Hebrews 5:11–14 (emphasis added)

These "milky" Christians are those folks who have become stagnant. They should be living in the destiny and wonder of the fullness of God's kingdom purposes. Instead they have regressed in maturity to being childish and unskilled in their faith. They become complainers and consumers. They require the kingdom of God to fit into their desires and agendas. This kind of consumerism is killing the North American church by dulling its senses, deceiving the church into believing that its needs are greater than the King's purposes.

A Word on Rest

An important posture for the believer to learn to engage is rest. Learning to rest will protect us from religion and burnout, but rest isn't stagnant. Often rest gets defined as stopping. This deception has given the enemy an opportunity to cause many believers to regress.

Rest is active, and in rest we move forward. Let me illustrate.

Roman warships, *triremes,* had both oars and sails. Imagine a *trireme* heading upriver, going against the current. If the oars and sails aren't used, the ship will drift backwards with the current. One way for it to move forward would be to force the slaves in the galley to begin to row. Rowing against the current requires twice the effort to go half the distance. As the slaves tire, they row slower and are only able to maintain a speed that counters the current, causing the ship to remain stationary.

However, if the crew were to hoist the sails, the wind would offer a greater power than the current. By using the wind, the ship could overcome the current and reach its destination. When the sails are full, the current loses its influence, because the direction of the current has no authority over the power of the wind.

This illustrates the concept of spiritual rest. To be stagnant in our faith is to allow the current of the world to push us back to former places or conditions. We can fight that current through committed religious rowing (works), and perhaps gain ground, but with exhausting effort. But like the slaves who tire, eventually our human effort can lead us to wearing out and feeling like all the effort we put into the rowing is in vain. I would like to suggest that rowing against the current causes burnout. Frustration and weariness overtake us and we just stop. I've seen this condition in believers often. And when they stop, they regress. Over and over again I hear people say that they wish their condition was like it was when they were doing better with God—"back then."

Remember the hunger I shared about at the beginning of the book? It kicks in here. We remember the scenery from when we were farther up the river. We remember how good it was, but remembering the effort we spent, remembering the exhaustion we felt in trying to go to the right place by using the wrong methods, makes us feel hopeless. So we stop, and yield our lives to the current. But we still have a hunger for more. Because of the old scenery around us, that hunger reminds our flesh of old pleasures, and we slip into sin.

Religion seems reasonable. Why? Because once we start walking with Jesus, we learn that the kingdom we are a part of is not of this world.

Jesus answered, "My kingdom is not of this world. If my kingdom were of this world, my servants would have been fighting, that I might not be delivered over to the Jews. But my kingdom is not from the world."
—John 18:36 (emphasis added)

We know that we are supposed to be different, and that we aren't supposed to flow with the current of the world. So we row, doing things that we feel will earn the Lord's favour and justify His sacrifice. This religious rowing is akin to using fleshly efforts to combat a spiritual issue.

However, like Jesus said, this is not a temporal kingdom; it's a kingdom of the Spirit. This was proved by the fact that Jesus' disciples weren't needed to protect Him. They wouldn't use a fleshly strategy to accomplish a spiritual goal.

So many Christians row and row. Then the enemy steps in with a tactic to trick them into thinking they should rest and stop rowing. But to stop is to drift backwards. Satan knows this and wins either way; either he has a tired religious Christian or a regressive one who's slipping back into old sinful ways.

This is how Christianity becomes boring to some. Their experience becomes like a journey up and down a portion of the river of God. They move forward to the end of their strength, give up, and then regress to old ways. They try this over and over, forward and back, getting wearier and more disinterested in the scenery because they've been there before. To them, moving forward in God equals boredom and exhaustion, and their hunger leads them to the short-term pleasure of their old fleshly passions, which leads them further and further from intimacy with the ever-increasing Heavenly Father. That is the way of religion.

There is a much better way: hoist the sails, find the wind, and let the sails do their work. Let me explain.

1. Hoist the Sails: Worship

The first step toward rest is worship. Worship commits us to a posture of upward focus. We lift up our heads (see Psalm 24) and allow the King of Glory to come in. We become immersed in His presence.

There is a new call to the body of Christ today. It's a call to value His presence over every other thing. No amount of work can make up for the lack of His presence. Remember when Moses told the Lord that the Promised Land wasn't going to have any worth without the presence of God?

And he said to him, "If your presence will not go with me, do not bring us up from here."

—Exodus 33:15

Unfortunately, many believers are accomplishing tasks for the King, but they're not walking in the presence of the King.

Religion wants you to work; God wants you to worship. Worship puts you in a position for the wind of the Spirit to propel you forward.

2. Find the Wind: Intimacy

Worship leads to intimacy. The second step toward rest is discovering which way the wind of the Spirit is blowing. The more intimate we are with God, the greater our capacity to hear His voice. He is speaking to us. But if we haven't postured ourselves in worship, we haven't created an atmosphere for intimacy.

I can't remember where I heard this, but if God has to shout, it means you're too far away. It seems that we have a tendency to want God to crack the skies open and make His directions clear. That, however, would remove faith from the equation.

People often ask how I know God is speaking. I always respond by saying that He has an accent. Wouldn't it be great if it was Scottish? You would hear in your heart that highland brogue and know that it's the voice of God! Well, it's not Scottish, but He has an accent: the accent of faith.

When God speaks, He always adds an element of faith to the task He has given us. Why? Because He is so *good*. Look at this scripture:

> *And without faith it is impossible to please him,* for whoever *would draw near to God must believe that he exists and that he rewards those who seek him.*
>
> —Hebrews 11:6 (emphasis added)

God, in His goodness, speaks to us in the accent of faith so that by choosing to engage obedience through faith, we please Him by default. He sets it up so that you please Him by obeying Him in faith. And it all starts by hearing His voice.

In other words, His voice will always lead you to an act of faith.

Intimacy creates a condition for us to hear the voice of God and set our sails in the direction His wind is blowing so we can engage the anointing.

3. Let the Sails Do Their Work: Anointing

And it shall come to pass in that day, that his burden shall be taken away from off thy shoulder, and his yoke from off thy neck, and the yoke shall be destroyed because of the anointing.

—Isaiah 10:27, KJV

The anointing of God comes to those who are on God's mission. The Holy Spirit is given to us as a pledge to empower us to do the work of God in His strength, not our own.

I may be working, but not in my strength; I work in His strength. I may get physically tired doing the work of the Lord, but I don't get spiritually weary because my energy doesn't come from my physical man; it comes from the anointing of the Spirit on my spirit.

And so, from the day we heard, we have not ceased to pray for you, asking that you may be filled with the knowledge of his will in all spiritual wisdom and understanding, so as to walk in a manner worthy of the Lord, fully pleasing to him: bearing fruit in every good work and increasing in the knowledge of God; being strengthened with all power, according to his glorious might, for all endurance and patience with joy; giving thanks to the Father, who has qualified you to share in the inheritance of the saints in light.

—Colossians 1:9–12 (emphasis added)

When we choose to walk in the anointing of the Holy Spirit, we are enlarging our capacity to do things for God because we are doing things in His strength instead of our own strength.

There is a futility in trying to accomplish the things of God through fleshly means. None of us have the capacity to heal without the Spirit. There are no words of knowledge, no wisdom, no prophecy, no miracles without the power of the Spirit. The best definition I have heard for religion came from Bill Johnson, who defined it as *form without power.* Religion is about doing things without the power of God... and it is exhausting.

For all the promises of God find their Yes in him. That is why it is through him that we utter our Amen to God for his glory. And it is God who establishes us with you in Christ, and has anointed us, and who has also put his seal on us and given us his Spirit in our hearts as a guarantee.

—2 Corinthians 1:20–22

When we walk with Jesus, we walk in the Spirit. When we set our spiritual sails, we are able to engage a power greater than us. The wind of the Spirit is stronger than the current of the world, enabling us to move forward in His strength, not ours.

That is rest. It is an active posture of reliance on the power of God to accomplish His purposes in and through our lives.

The Arm of the Flesh

With him is an arm of flesh, but with us is the Lord our God, to help us and to fight our battles." And the people took confidence from the words of Hezekiah king of Judah.

—2 Chronicles 32:8 (emphasis added)

In the course of learning how to rest, you're going to discover that there are times when being obedient to the Lord feels like rowing, which means you're operating in the flesh and not the anointing.

My friend and hunting buddy, Ed, who is one of my church's elders, recently attended a teaching I gave on the subject of rest. He pointed out brilliantly that it is okay to lift your oars in one area if the sails are full in others. The point is this: once the process of learning to rest in the Him has begun, God will use energy loss to show where you're in the anointing and where you're using the arm of the flesh. The good news is that if you're engaging the wind in some of the areas, you can lift the oars in others and learn whether you need to realign yourself with God's purposes to be free from burnout and maintain an even keel, a life of kingdom order.

To have an even keel, the weight of a ship's cargo must be evenly distributed. This helps the ship sail efficiently by staying in balance. In our lives, once we're clear on how to rest, we are better able to bring order to our activities based on the level of anointing we possess to accomplish the work before us. We can also discern the activities which we have an anointing for versus the areas where we work in our own strength.

God, in His great grace, allows us to bring order to our lives by using the current of the world. He takes what Satan would use to restrain us and uses it to refine us.

Come to me, all who labor and are heavy laden, and I will give you rest. Take my yoke upon you, and learn from me, for I am gentle and lowly in heart, and you will find rest for your souls. For my yoke is easy, and my burden is light.

—Matthew 11:28–30

Jesus spoke these comforting words to a crowd that was labouring under an oppressive religious yoke. His invitation is to be yoked to Him, and in that connection of intimacy we will find the rest that eludes us. It's not found in stopping, but in stillness; it is not silent, it is quiet; it is not busy, it is active; it is not tiring, but it takes effort. His rest is a place where striving ceases and intimacy increases. Resting in the work of Christ is absolutely beautiful.

Worship hoists the sails, intimacy helps us find the direction of the wind, and the anointing does the work.

Now that we've established the value of growth, let's begin to explore the foundation of the ancient pillars. First off, we'll look at the elementary doctrines of Jesus.

chapter six

Elementary School

Therefore let us leave the elementary doctrine of Christ and go on to maturity, not laying again a foundation of repentance from dead works and of faith toward God, and of instruction about washings, the laying on of hands, the resurrection of the dead, and eternal judgement.

—Hebrews 6:1–2

As I began searching for clarity about these pillars that hold up an open heaven, I felt led to visit this passage in Hebrews 6. In it, we find the six elementary doctrines of Christ.

1. Repentance from dead works.
2. Faith toward God.
3. Instruction about washings (baptism).
4. The laying on of hands.
5. The resurrection of the dead.
6. Eternal judgement.

These look pretty heady to me, yet the writer of Hebrews considers them to be elementary. In other words, he's saying, "Let's leave elementary school, not living only in the foundations but building *on* the foundations."

These elementary doctrines hold great value for us as disciples, but they are elementary. They are foundational, and there is more beyond them.

Most of us remember the three R's: reading, writing, and arithmetic. Learning to read is necessary (foundational) to later be able to read deeper concepts. We use what we have learned to help us learn more. Understanding compound sentences started with understanding simple sentences. Understanding algebraic functions started with understanding simple arithmetic.

Just like our educational foundations prepare us to capture greater knowledge, so too do the elementary doctrines of Christ prepare the way for us to gain deeper knowledge of His kingdom. We must establish the elementary doctrines to mature in our revelation of His greatness. But to mature, we must build on those doctrines, not live there.

Our doctrine must mature. Our experience with His nature must increase. Our passion for Him must grow beyond foundational doctrines about Him. As disciples, we have a responsibility to grow to full maturity so we can move forward rather than backward.

Through the elementary doctrines, we are enabled to walk in greater things.

I'm going to briefly look at each of these elementary doctrines. I'll first take a moment to describe the doctrine and then discuss why it's foundational.

1. Repentance from Dead Works

The Greek word repentance is *metanioa*, which means the reversal of a decision. Essentially, this doctrine is the reversal of the decision that works will establish favour with God. It is the rejection of religion, which is why it's linked with the next doctrine (faith toward God).

This doctrine is foundational because it points us to the fact that we are saved by grace, not by works. It's also important to note that the author is writing to the Hebrews, a people whose understanding of God was rooted in their religious traditions and practices. It would have been earth-shattering for them to be told that those practices no longer held value in light of the cross. All that these Hebrews knew was a God of tradition and sacrifice. They believed that atonement and forgiveness had to be purchased (through sacrificial animals).

Interestingly, the Hebrews wouldn't have struggled with wondering about forgiveness as a modern-day Christian would. They would have just done the work of the sacrifice. Faith was not a part of their equation. They knew what to do to make things right with God. Now they were released from the religious yoke of oppression and brought into this key understanding:

> *For by grace you* have been saved through faith. And this is not your own doing; *it is the gift of God, not a result of works, so that no one may boast.*
>
> —Ephesians 2:8–9 (emphasis added)

This would have been hard for them. Their relationship with God was now about grace and faith, and no longer works. Their entire religious system of works returning them to right standing was done away with; a new covenant based in grace and faith was established.

I think it's important to consider the nature of the Pharisees in light of Ephesians 2:8–9. Jesus made it clear that the religious leaders of the day were proud of their position and piety. The more "holy" they were on account of their religious practices, the more important they were and the worthier they were of respect and honour. While it's important to walk with a sense of honour for our leaders, these leaders felt they had earned their honour because of how religious they were. Paul, a former *"Hebrew of the Hebrews"* (Philippians 3:4–6), who would have been familiar with this pride. He writes that our salvation isn't our own doing; rather it's a gift because of God's grace—His *charis* (favour) toward us.

Through the once-and-for-all sacrifice of Jesus, salvation came to the Hebrews as a gift by the grace and love of God. This truth remains for the Hebrews and for us today. No amount of religious activity can earn our salvation; it has been graciously given to us, should we choose to receive it.

2. Faith Toward God

Repentance from dead works and faith toward God are connected, and their connection unlocks an important truth about repentance. Repentance requires us to embrace one thought over another. When we change our minds, we are not in stasis. Moving from one perspective requires us to embrace another. Somehow in Christianity we have developed a post-repentance stasis during which we confess sin and repent for it but don't move toward God and embrace a changed perspective on the issue.

Here's why this doctrine is foundational in our faith. I wrote earlier that we are not to blame for being deceived by a lie, that a fish doesn't bite a hook knowingly. However, those who don't engage this foundational principle actually do bite hooks, and they know that they're biting hooks.

Many of the redeemed live in a cycle, trapped in sin that recurs over and over again. It's a cycle of temptation, sin, confession, and repentance. The cycle continues, and they feel like there is no end, no freedom, and that they will face an angry God over their willful sin. They know that it's wrong, but at a deep level they aren't convinced that He is sufficient for them, so they try to add to their lack in Him with sinful activity. The foundational truth of faith toward God, following repentance, protects us from turning *from* and returning *to* our sin.

> When you repent, you turn from sin, but you *must* turn to God or you'll return to the sin. Turn or return, there is no rest in a sin-cycle-filled life.

When you repent, you turn from sin, but you *must* turn to God or you'll return to the sin. Turn or return, there is no rest in a sin-cycle-filled life.

The Work of Repentance vs. the Fruit of Repentance. John the Baptist declared to the Pharisees, *"Bear fruit in keeping with repentance"* (Matthew 3:8). They were coming to his baptism when he demonstrated the difference between the work of repentance and the fruit of repentance.

We recently hosted a healing conference with Dr. Randy Clark, the leader of Global Awakening. Dr. Clark was part of the revival at Toronto Airport Vineyard. He shared a thought that fits directly with this foundational principle of turn or return. He said that it is the work of repentance to realize, through the conviction of the Holy Spirit, that you have been going in the wrong direction and change your mind and turn around. It is the fruit of repentance to choose to walk in the opposite direction toward the Lord's alternative. John declares that we need to bear fruit in keeping with repentance.

No Rest for the Rebel. The post-repentance stasis leads to the hardening of our hearts. A hardened heart is a heart that's no longer able to be moulded and shaped by God. It's a rebellious heart that wants its own way. It's being a natural man, at a point when the former things it knew of God seem like foolishness. The hardened heart will not forgive, remains jealous, judges, and never finds rest in God. Why? Because it makes a place for sin. It is compartmentalized, and it is compromised.

> *Take care, brothers, lest there be in any of you* an evil, unbelieving heart, leading you to fall away from the living God. *But exhort one another every day, as long as it is called "today," that* none of you may be hardened by the deceitfulness of sin. *For we have come to share in Christ, if indeed we hold our original confidence firm to the end. As it is said, "Today, if you hear his voice,* do not harden your hearts as in the rebellion. *"*
>
> *For who were those who heard and yet rebelled? Was it not all those who left Egypt led by Moses? And with whom was he provoked for forty years? Was it not with those who sinned, whose bodies fell in the wilderness? And to whom did he swear that they would not enter his rest, but to those who were disobedient? So we see that they were unable to enter because of unbelief.*
>
> *Therefore,* while the promise of entering his rest still stands, let us fear lest any of you should seem to have failed to reach it.
>
> —Hebrews 3:12–4:1 (emphasis added)

These are the hearts of the religious who judge and wound their brothers and sisters in Christ and leave a bitter taste in the mouths of the lost on account of their joyless hypocrisy. Hardened hearts are the result of not submitting to the foundation of faith toward God. It is an ungodly form of repentance that thinks words and works will satisfy God, rather than faith and grace, and it results in dead religious duty as opposed to living relational intimacy. One leads to works; the other leads to rest.

The term post-repentance stasis is best defined by the Apostle Paul as worldly grief:

> *For godly grief produces a repentance that leads to salvation without regret, whereas worldly grief produces death.*
>
> —2 Corinthians 7:10

It is the difference between feeling sorrow for sinning and feeling sorrow for being caught sinning, which shows whether we have merely succumbed to temptation or harboured a sinful condition in our hearts.

Repentance: A Gateway to a Transformed Life. Turning from our sin toward God provides a gateway to transformation. This is the start of renovating our minds. Completing our act of repentance allows us to engage heaven's perspective on the area of our repentance.

Let's say you find yourself harbouring unforgiveness toward someone. Through whatever means, the Holy Spirit convicts you according to righteousness and you realize that you're sinning by walking in unforgiveness. So you confess it as sin, and then you repent. Then you turn with faith toward the Lord. That's how repentance becomes a gateway to renovating our minds.

By turning to the Lord, through both the Word of God and intimacy with Jesus, we learn His perspective on forgiveness. Here is a biblical example:

> *Then Peter came up and said to him, "Lord, how often will my brother sin against me, and I forgive him? As many as seven times?"*
>
> *Jesus said to him, "I do not say to you seven times, but seventy-seven times."*
>
> —Matthew 18:21–22

Once we repent, the gateway is open for us to understand heaven's perspective on forgiveness. Then we can set our minds on the things that are above (Colossians 3:2). This causes us to renovate our way of thinking and renew our minds.

So in the future when an offence gives us an opportunity to walk in unforgiveness, we can engage our new heavenly mindset on forgiveness and respond out of our conviction rather than reacting to the issue at hand in a fleshly way.

While there's a miraculous element to the transformation that takes place in our lives, it's comforting to know that I have a part to play in hastening that miracle by renovating my thoughts and engaging the perspective of heaven.

Romans 8:28 promises that all things will work together for good for us who are called according to God's purpose. His purpose is for His Kingdom ways to be established here on earth through us. Even Satan's attacks, when stewarded properly through confession and repentance, can be used to bring us closer to God. This is why no weapon formed against us prospers (Isaiah 54:17). Think of it this way: as with the cross, Satan's grand scheme for destruction turned out to be the vehicle for his own destruction. God, being able to take what the devil does and turn it to good, uses our repentance as a way for us to renovate our thinking and never be stuck in bondage to that issue again.

Whom the son sets free is free indeed. Yes, God!

A Word on Freedom. Jesus has entirely purchased our freedom, and we can ask for forgiveness and return to intimacy with Him. But we have a responsibility to maintain our freedom.

I love fishing. Most fishermen will tell you that they have a favourite hook, and I'm no different. My favourite hook is a Len Thompson Red Devil. It's a white spoon-style hook with a red stripe down the middle. I can catch fish in a puddle with one of those hooks! (Okay, that's a fisherman's tale right there.) It is my favourite hook.

The devil knows which hook you'll bite on. That will be the one he throws your way over and over again. It's a sin that easily entangles us—in a sense, Satan's favourite hook for you.

Therefore, since we have so great a cloud of witnesses surrounding us,
let us also lay aside every encumbrance and the sin which so

easily entangles us, *and let us run with endurance the race that is set before us...*

—Hebrews 12:1, NASB (emphasis added)

I once saw a painting of a gladiator running for his life in the arena. Behind him, a huge male lion lunged with his mouth in a snarl and his claws reaching toward the retreating gladiator. The caption said "Sometimes second place is not good enough."

Immediately the Lord asked me, "Landen, what would have been the best strategy for that gladiator?"

Knowing that God doesn't ask a question to learn the answer, I replied, "I don't know. What do You think?"

His response was telling. "He should have avoided the arena."

Avoid the arena. What a novel thought!

My point is this. Some temptations are specific to a location. Much of the enemy's easy fishing can be avoided by simply avoiding unsafe environments. Do you struggle with gossip? Don't go near the group when you hear them start. Pornography? Keep yourself away from the internet when you know you're weak. Swearing? Quit playing hockey. You know, avoid the arena!

Be sober-minded; be watchful. Your adversary the devil prowls around like a roaring lion, seeking someone to devour.

—1 Peter 5:8

My dad's favourite joke is the one where the patient comes into the doctor's office saying that he had broken his leg in three places. The doctor replies, "You should stay away from those places."

Great freedom will come when you're able to confidently stand before the Lord knowing that you've avoided the deliberate temptation of the enemy in an area of your personal weakness. Remember the phrase "Temptation has location." It will help you avoid those weaknesses.

Fight to win. Don't enter into an arena with a lion you aren't confident you can beat. Satan will never enter a field of battle without stacking the odds in his favour. He'll always try to intimidate and demoralize

you by sending Goliath. That was the
massive tactical error on Saul's part in
1 Samuel 17. He let Goliath set the
terms of the battle. The enemy does

Fight to win.

the same. He sets up the arena so you'll fall. The devil hates you. He has
no sense of honour in battle. His hatred will never permit him to create
a battle scenario that gives his opponent any hope of victory, let alone
an edge. He'll set mines on the battlefield and present a champion, an
opponent who cannot be slain through any natural means. He'll stop at
nothing and stoop to any low to ensure his victory.

Here's the good news: since Jesus redeemed us, we don't have to step
foot into any arena devised by the devil. The great deceiver was entirely deceived through the cross and has lost all authority to set the terms
of battle! Jesus has already won and we are victorious! I never let the
devil set the terms for the conflict. I set them according to heaven's rule
of engagement, which says that I am more than a conqueror (Romans
8:37). Being more than a conqueror means not engaging from a point of
weakness, or from a place of equality. It means attacking from a position
of strength. In fact, it's more than that; it's attacking from a position of
dominance! That's what avoiding the location of temptation looks like.
It's entering the battle as a champion, a victor, not as a veal cutlet. Don't
set yourself up to be lunch for a lion.

Temptation has location. Now that's a renovated thought!

The next elementary truth empowers us to live in that position of
dominance.

3. Instruction on Washings (Baptism)

The next elementary principle has to do with baptism. Understanding
what baptism represents, and what it legally accomplishes in the realm of
the spirit, enables us to live with dominance over the enemy.

*What shall we say then? Are we to continue in sin that grace may
abound? By no means!* How can we who died to sin still live in
it? *Do you not know that all of us who have been baptized into Christ*

Jesus were baptized into his death? We were buried therefore with him by baptism into death, in order that, just as Christ was raised from the dead by the glory of the Father, we too might walk in newness of life.

For if we have been united with him in a death like his, we shall certainly be united with him in a resurrection like his. We know that our old self was crucified *with him in order that the* body of sin *might be brought to nothing, so that we would* no longer be enslaved to sin. *For one who has died has been* set free from sin.

—Romans 6:1–7 (emphasis added)

Baptism is more than a public declaration of faith in Christ. It is also a public execution of the sin nature we inherited from Adam.

Therefore, just as sin came into the world through one man, *and* death through sin, and so death spread to all men *because all sinned…*

—Romans 5:12 (emphasis added)

A necessary shift must come to our thinking with regard to baptism, especially in the evangelical and charismatic movements. For some reason, we have begun to embrace a nonbiblical point of view. We've created a culture that says that people can be baptized when they're mature enough.

While it's important that a person understands what they're doing when they get baptized, it's a part of their salvation process, not their discipleship.

I think the apostles would be confused as to why we wait to be baptized. If you search through the Scriptures, new converts were baptized immediately. Why? Because baptism gives us our first miraculous encounter with God, in that our sin nature is miraculously put to death and we rise into resurrection life.

Baptism is one's first act of covenant partnership. I often say to my church that Jesus took the cross and we take a bath. Think of it this way: we use debit cards to access our bank accounts instead of using cash. When you get a debit card, you have to activate it to be able to access your funds.

In the same way, baptism activates the power of the covenant for believers, giving them full access to all that they've inherited through Jesus.

I'm not about to start an argument about whether you're saved or not if you haven't been baptized, but I do believe that kingdom activation lies in wait for those who haven't submitted to the waters of baptism.

Baptism is a legal separation from the body of sin (Romans 6:6). In ancient times, wars were brutal. There was no Geneva Convention to direct the world's armies to treat prisoners of war decently. One particularly heinous form of torture was to strap a dead body from the battlefield onto the back of a captured soldier. This would cause a horrifically slow death due to the decay of the dead body. Paul uses this example of the body of sin to illustrate the condition of a believer who hasn't been baptized. It's like living with a dead old man strapped to us. Baptism separates us from our old nature so we can fully put on the new.

Not a Reset Button. We need to understand that being born again isn't just a reset button that wipes us clean from sin.

I have to admit that I'm a bit of an Apple product junkie. I own a MacBook and an iPad as well as an iPhone. Somewhere I have an iPod as well. Don't judge me! When I want to sync one of these devices with my computer, there's an option to reset it to factory settings. That means I can reset my iPod to the original manufactured condition. So if I feel like it's gotten cluttered, I can start all over again and reload it in the way I want.

When man was created by God, he was created in His likeness.

Then God said, "Let us make man in our image, after our likeness. *And let them have dominion over the fish of the sea and over the birds of the heavens and over the livestock and over all the earth and over every creeping thing that creeps on the earth."*

So God created man in his own image, *in the image of God he created him; male and female he created them.*

—Genesis 1:26–27 (emphasis added)

When we are born again, we aren't returned to our condition at birth, still possessing a sin nature. We are returned to the pre-fall nature of Adam. Look at what Paul wrote to the Ephesians:

...to put off your old self, which belongs to your former manner of life and is corrupt through deceitful desires, and to be renewed in the spirit of your minds, and to put on the new self, created after the likeness of God *in true righteousness and holiness.*

—Ephesians 4:22–24 (emphasis added)

When we are born again, we aren't returned to our condition at birth, still possessing a sin nature. We are returned to the pre-fall nature of Adam.

The new self won't fit very well with the old man strapped to us. It's like putting a wetsuit on over SCUBA gear. This is why the new walk doesn't seem to fit for some believers, or they struggle to walk in newness of life with Jesus because they can't fully let go of their past.

Baptism addresses Satan's legal right to man by bringing the body of sin to nothing, giving us the legal condition of being born again. That's why baptism is part of the great commission. Through baptism, we are totally set free, both to leave the past behind and enter into the promises of God and the gifts He has for us.

4. The Laying on of Hands

While baptism is foundational in initiating an individual's transformation, the laying on of hands initiates the transference of spiritual things. In the Old Testament, the laying on of hands had two basic functions: blessings and curses. Here are a couple of examples.

Jacob was reunited with his son Joseph and blessed Joseph's sons:

And Joseph took them both, Ephraim in his right hand toward Israel's left hand, and Manasseh in his left hand toward Israel's right hand, and brought them near him.

—Genesis 48:13

In a second example, the high priest, through the atonement process under the law, laid hands on a goat and put upon it the sins of the nation.

He then released the goat into the wilderness. By this act, the goat was made to carry the curse of the nation's sin, and the nation was separated from its sin.

> *And when he has made an end of atoning for the Holy Place and the tent of meeting and the altar, he shall present the live goat.* And Aaron shall lay both his hands on the head of the live goat, and confess over it all the iniquities of the people of Israel, and all their transgressions, all their sins. *And he shall put them on the head of the goat and send it away into the wilderness by the hand of a man who is in readiness. The goat shall bear all their iniquities on itself to a remote area, and he shall let the goat go free in the wilderness.*
> —Leviticus 16:20–22 (emphasis added)

Our New Covenant experience is wonderfully different. The purpose of the laying on of hands is to release others into their destiny. Observe this moment between the Apostle Paul and Timothy:

> *I am reminded of your sincere faith, a faith that dwelt first in your grandmother Lois and your mother Eunice and now, I am sure, dwells in you as well. For this reason I remind you to* fan into flame the gift of God, which is in you through the laying on of my hands, *for God gave us a spirit not of fear but of power and love and self-control.*
> —2 Timothy 1:5–7 (emphasis added)

We see here that the laying on of hands transfers the gift of God from Paul to Timothy, and Timothy is encouraged to fan it into flame. Under the Old Covenant, fathers passed on their spiritual blessing and family anointing to the eldest son. The blessing was to be released to the eldest son in the father's bloodline. The other children received an inheritance and blessing, but it paled in comparison to what the eldest received.

Consider the terms bloodline and position in the bloodline. Let that sink in. You had to be in the family, and your birth order determined your rank and the level of your blessing.

In Genesis 15, Abram lamented before the Lord about his lack of an heir. He had no one in his bloodline, no son to receive his anointing and blessing. However, the exclusivity of the Old Covenant family has been replaced with the inclusivity of the New Covenant of faith through the work of Jesus.

> *But now that faith has come, we are no longer under a guardian, for in Christ Jesus* you are all sons of God, through faith. *For as many of you as were baptized into Christ have put on Christ. There is neither Jew nor Greek, there is neither slave nor free, there is no male and female,* for you are all one in Christ Jesus. *And if you are Christ's, then you are Abraham's offspring, heirs according to promise.*
> —Galatians 3:25–29 (emphasis added)

The good news of our New Covenant experience is that salvation grafts into the family line, so all members are part of the family of God!

Paul reminded Timothy that he had released a gift from God by laying hands on him. He tells Timothy to fan it into flame. This shows us that the spiritual blessings we receive can be given away to others in the family.

John Wimber, the founder of the Vineyard movement, used to say, "Everyone gets to play." That means that no one is left out of the blessing of God and the blessing of being used by God. Let me explain.

The Firstborn Who Shares. Jesus is the firstborn son of all.

> *He is the image of the invisible God, the* firstborn of all creation. *For by him all things were created, in heaven and on earth, visible and invisible, whether thrones or dominions or rulers or authorities*—all things were created through him and for him. *And he is before all things, and in him all things hold together. And he is the head of the body, the church.* He is the beginning, the firstborn from the dead, that in everything he might be preeminent. *For in him all the fullness of God was pleased to dwell, and through him to reconcile to himself all things, whether on earth or in heaven, making peace by the blood of his cross.*
> —Colossians 1:15–20 (emphasis added)

Jesus wasn't lacking authority when He came to earth. Mankind was. The victory of the cross wasn't a victory for God. In the wink of an eye, He could have destroyed the enemy and all his works. The cross was a victory for mankind. The cross returned mankind's authority to what it was intended to be in the first place.

Jesus didn't win a victory for Himself. He won a victory for us. There was no concern in the Godhead or in the mind of Jesus as to the power of death over Him. There was no chance that He might not make it. In fact, it's baffling how the great deceiver was so completely deceived. Satan must have really believed death could contain the all-powerful God!

For this reason the Father loves me, because I lay down my life that I may take it up again. No one takes it from me, but I lay it down of my own accord. I have authority to lay it down, and I have authority to take it up again. This charge I have received from my Father.
—John 10:17–18 (emphasis added)

Jesus laid down His life with every intention of picking it up again. He was given the authority by the Father to do that very thing. The game plan of heaven was executed to perfection.

One of the lies the enemy has managed to slip into the psyche of man is that the cross was a lucky break, a fluky goal in an overtime win where the underdog managed to surprise the odds-on favourite.

Nothing could be further from the truth!

The cross wasn't a fortunate victory scraped out by an unlikely victor. It was, and remains, an overwhelming defeat over a toothless fraud who had no business being in the same arena as our champion, Jesus! In fact, this opponent (and I use the term loosely) was and is so monumentally outclassed that he was convinced that scoring on himself would bring victory.

This was not a fight for the ages. This was an overwhelming victory of such alarming proportions that the enemy will forever wear its shame.

In sport, there is losing bad, and there is losing ugly. Satan did both.

There is a tradition amongst some Orthodox churches on Easter Monday to tell jokes, the reason being that the cosmic joke of the devil trying to kill Jesus is so ridiculously funny that the body of Christ should respond by laughing throughout the first day of resurrection life.

Recently, I was speaking at a youth camp and mentioned this to the teens. I then told them the resurrection joke, saying, "Remember the one about the devil when he tried to kill Jesus?"

And we all started laughing and laughing and it was glorious. At the end of the week, we had baptisms and a young lady got up and testified as to the change the week had brought to her and how she had been saved and was excited to be baptized. She shared how she had struggled with fear for years and how it had paralyzed her. Then she declared that she had been set free from fear through the power of the cross and said, "Because, you know, remember the one about how the devil tried to kill Jesus?"

And then we all laughed and laughed.

Why do the nations rage and the peoples plot in vain? The kings of the earth set themselves, and the rulers take counsel together, against the Lord and against his Anointed, saying, "Let us burst their bonds apart and cast away their cords from us."

He who sits in the heavens laughs; the Lord holds them in derision.

—Psalms 2:1–4

The cross could never end the reign of the King.

In the end, Jesus showed us what a Christian should look like. Jesus came to earth as a man with a mind set on heaven, filled with the Spirit, and extending the kingdom of God.

What does this have to do with the laying on of hands? The nature of His victory *for us* has released His power *to us*. He is the firstborn of mankind but chooses to share His inheritance with us.

For you did not receive the spirit of slavery to fall back into fear, but you have received the Spirit of adoption as sons, by whom we cry, "Abba! Father!" The Spirit himself bears witness with our spirit that we are children of God, and if children, then heirs—heirs of God and fellow heirs with Christ, *provided we suffer with him in order that we may also be glorified with him.*

—Romans 8:15–17 (emphasis added)

Again in Galatians:

For as many of you as were baptized into Christ have put on Christ. There is neither Jew nor Greek, there is neither slave nor free, there is no male and female, for you are all one in Christ Jesus. And if you are Christ's, then you are Abraham's offspring, heirs according to promise.

—Galatians 3:27–29 (emphasis added)

He is the firstborn who shares His inheritance with us! The inheritance is eternal life in heaven and authority over the works of darkness on earth. That promised inheritance was given through Christ and guaranteed by the gift of the Holy Spirit. Jesus gave us back authority and the anointing we were originally intended to walk in and then charged us to give that anointing to others through the laying on of hands.

In the New Covenant experience, the laying on of hands is a transfer of blessing and grace, power and healing, and the baptism of the Holy Spirit, not just on account of positional favour but because Jesus took His inheritance and shared it with us, so we can share it with others.

You and I are both a part of the family and our position in the family has been secured by a beloved firstborn Son who has shared the bounty of His Father's inheritance with us. Through the laying on of hands, we are able to release the promise of the inheritance to come, the Holy Spirit, to one another... and everybody gets to play.

5. Resurrection of the Dead and Eternal Judgement

Up until now, the elementary doctrines of Jesus have dealt with supernatural release through our natural form. In other words, our lives are a preview of what it will be like when His kingdom comes. There will come a day, however, a glorious day, when faith will be replaced with finality.

The King will rule and reign here on earth and establish His kingdom in the seen realm, and death will no longer be a necessity for mankind.

Like repentance and faith toward God, these last two elementary principles are connected. I'll address them separately and then write about how they are connected.

The resurrection of the dead has three components. First, at the core of Christianity, is the resurrection of Jesus, which is the foundation of our faith. Second is the assurance of all who believe that there is life beyond the grave. Third, the resurrection of all the dead, and all mankind, will be part of the White Throne Judgement.

1 Corinthians 15 shows all three aspects:

> *Now if Christ is proclaimed as raised from the dead, how can some of you say that there is no resurrection of the dead? But if there is no resurrection of the dead, then not even Christ has been raised. And if Christ has not been raised, then our preaching is in vain and your faith is in vain. We are even found to be misrepresenting God, because we testified about God that he raised Christ, whom he did not raise if it is true that the dead are not raised. For if the dead are not raised, not even Christ has been raised. And if Christ has not been raised, your faith is futile and you are still in your sins. Then those also who have fallen asleep in Christ have perished. If in Christ we have hope in this life only, we are of all people most to be pitied.*
>
> *But in fact Christ has been raised from the dead, the firstfruits of those who have fallen asleep. For as by a man came death, by a man has come also the resurrection of the dead. For as in Adam all die, so also in Christ shall all be made alive. But each in his own order: Christ the firstfruits, then at his coming those who belong to Christ. Then comes the end, when he delivers the kingdom to God the Father after destroying every rule and every authority and power.*
>
> —1 Corinthians 15:12–24 (emphasis added)

Absent but Alive. Paul shows us that believers who have died are in the presence of God.

for we walk by faith, not by sight. Yes, we are of good courage, and we would rather be away from the body and at home with the Lord. *So whether we are at home or away, we make it our aim to please him.*
—2 Corinthians 5:7–9 (emphasis added)

For to me to live is Christ, and to die is gain. If I am to live in the flesh, that means fruitful labor for me. Yet which I shall choose I cannot tell. I am hard pressed between the two. My desire is to depart and be with Christ, for that is far better. *But to remain in the flesh is more necessary on your account.*
—Philippians 1:21–24 (emphasis added)

But he also contends that believers will have new bodies at the second coming of Jesus.

For as in Adam all die, so also in Christ shall all be made alive. *But each in his own order: Christ the firstfruits,* then at his coming those who belong to Christ.
—1 Corinthians 15:22–23 (emphasis added)

That departure into the realm of the Spirit is for both those who believe and those who don't believe. One gets to be present with Jesus; the other does not. This is the gift and the weapon of death.

Death: A Gift and a Weapon. Earlier I shared about Satan's monumental oversight with regard to killing Jesus. Satan was duped when he thought he could use death as a weapon to destroy Jesus. His mistake was that he thought having the authority to use the weapon was the same as having authority over the weapon.

In Alberta, you can start to drive on your own at sixteen. One day, shortly after my son earned his driver's license, he announced that he was going to take the van to run an errand for himself. I replied that he wasn't able to do that because I was going to need the van.

"What do you need the van for?" he demanded.

Fortunately, I was in a good mood.

I informed him that if I wanted to, I could open the garage door, start the van up, and rev it for a few moments while eating a sandwich, no matter how urgent his errand was. I had authority over the van and he had authority to use it… occasionally.

Satan doesn't have authority over death; he only has the authority to use it, and he is brutal in his use of death. He will use any and every means to steal, kill, and destroy. That is why we must urgently love the world, because our enemy *"prowls around like a roaring lion, seeking someone to devour"* (1 Peter 5:8).

> *But we do not want you to be uninformed, brothers, about those who are asleep, that you may not grieve as others do who have no hope.*
> —1 Thessalonians 4:13

It's important that we have a healthy understanding of death.

Before discussing this further, note that the purpose of this book is not to debate the sovereignty of God or affirm or disprove any doctrinal perspective on death. I will not try to present any explanation for why some die when they do or who is responsible. What I do wish to present is a freeing perspective on death for the believer and bring the sober truth to the unbeliever.

The Gift. Satan didn't create death. God did. God created it so that man wouldn't be stuck living eternally in his fallen state. Death was not part of the original condition of creation. However, man's disobedience meant that there needed to be a way for the flesh and the spirit to be separated so that man could be returned to open fellowship with God.

I want to say it again: Satan did not create death. He has no creative power (the ability to create something from nothing), only a capacity to pervert. God, in His grace, provided a way out of us having to live forever with sin as master over us.

This is why death to the believer is a gift. No matter what form it may come in, death will always be a doorway to face-to-face fellowship with Jesus. It will never separate us from God. In the flesh, He is with us in Spirit, and in death we are with Him in spirit. Either way, we are together with Him, never separated, because we were born of the spirit before the death of the flesh.

Which is why death can also be a weapon.

That which is born of the flesh is flesh, and that which is born of the Spirit is spirit.

—John 3:6

The Weapon. Dying and perishing are two different things.

And just as it is appointed for man to die once, and after that comes judgement...

—Hebrews 9:27

The Greek word for die is *apothnesko*. It's a compound word, with *apo* denoting a departure and *thnesko* meaning simply to die.

The Lord is not slow to fulfill his promise as some count slowness, but is patient toward you, not wishing that any should perish, *but that all should reach repentance.*

—2 Peter 3:9 (emphasis added)

For God so loved the world, that he gave his only Son, that whoever believes in him should not perish *but have eternal life.*

—John 3:16 (emphasis added)

The word perish is the Greek word *apollymi*. It is also a compound word, with *apo* again denoting departure and *olethros* meaning destruction and punishment.

No matter what form it may take, death to the unbeliever is a weapon of the enemy because it will separate them from the love of God. Forever.

For those who believe, death cannot be used as a weapon. Whether premature or not, peaceful or painful, when death comes to the believer, it bears the gift of instantaneous fellowship with Jesus, because those born of the spirit are able to be present in the spirit. However, considering that death's timeline is unknown, if it arrives before someone makes the decision to confess and engage the lordship of Jesus, before being born again, death becomes a weapon of great destruction, bringing with it the consequence of hell.

One dies, the other perishes.

Connecting the Dots. Here is the connection between the two doctrines. The dead will be raised and mankind will be judged.

There are two judgements, one for believers and one for unbelievers. They are referred to as the Judgement Seat of Christ (or the Bema Seat) and the White Throne Judgement.

Before we go into these judgements, bear in mind that I hold to a premillennial doctrinal view. This book isn't meant to be a defence of that view, nor should it affect my perspective on the connection between this elementary doctrine and its connection with the ancient pillars which we'll discuss further.

The Judgement Seat of Christ (The Bema Seat)

When Will it Happen? The Judgement Seat of Christ will happen after the rapture of the saints and the first resurrection, where we will all be given glorified bodies.

> *For this we declare to you by a word from the Lord, that we who are alive, who are left until the coming of the Lord, will not precede those who have fallen asleep. For the Lord himself will descend from heaven with a cry of command, with the voice of an archangel, and with the* sound of the trumpet of God. And the dead in Christ will rise first. Then we who are alive, who are left, will be caught up together with them in the clouds to meet the Lord in the air, *and so we will always be with the Lord. Therefore encourage one another with these words.*
>
> —1 Thessalonians 4:15–18 (emphasis added)

> *I tell you this, brothers:* flesh and blood cannot inherit the kingdom of God, *nor does the perishable inherit the imperishable. Behold!*

I tell you a mystery. We shall not all sleep, but we shall all be changed, *in a moment, in the twinkling of an eye, at the last trumpet.* For the *tru*mpet will sound, and the dead will be raised imperishable, *and we shall be changed.* For this perishable body must put on the imperishable, and this mortal body must put on immortality. *When the perishable puts on the imperishable, and the mortal puts on immortality, then shall come to pass the saying that is written: "Death is swallowed up in victory." "O death, where is your victory? O death, where is your sting?"*

—1 Corinthians 15:50–55 (emphasis added)

What Will Happen? Every believer will stand before the Lord and their lives will be examined. Their efforts will be tested by fire and that test will determine the reward they are given.

For we must all appear *before the judgement seat of Christ, so that each one may* receive what is due *for what he has done in the body,* whether good or evil.

—2 Corinthians 5:10 (emphasis added)

For no one can lay a foundation other than that which is laid, which is Jesus Christ. Now if anyone builds on the foundation with gold, silver, precious stones, wood, hay, straw—each one's work will become manifest, for the Day will disclose it, because it will be revealed by fire, and the fire will test what sort of work each one has done. *If the work that anyone has built on the foundation survives, he will receive a reward. If anyone's* work is burned up, he will suffer loss, *though he himself will be saved, but only as through fire.*

—1 Corinthians 3:11–15 (emphasis added)

This judgement can seem daunting, but there are a couple of important things we as believers need to understand. I used to think that all my deeds, good and evil, would be revealed and I would be embarrassed in front of the heavenly host for all the things I have done wrong—all my sin and shame displayed for all of heaven to see. Boy, was I wrong.

Jesus came and lived a perfect, sinless life on our behalf so that He could be our representative in covenant with God. Our choice to believe in Him as Lord and Saviour positions us under the covenant of God.

My sin has been judged on the cross. I am free from the judgement of sin. As a believer, I have chosen to let Jesus be the sin payment on my behalf. Those of us who have chosen Christ have had our sins covered under the blood of Jesus.

This is a place for reward. Paul used language to help the Corinthians understand the wonder of the mo-

> My sin has been judged on the cross. I am free from the judgement of sin.

ment. The Bema Seat was a place in the city square where rewards were given to athletes and where justice awarded to people. By using this term, Paul made it clear that it can be a great place. Paul's language sometimes gets confused in our modern translations. We read in 2 Corinthians 5:10 that we will receive what is due to us for what we have done, *whether good or evil*. The Greek word *phaulos* does mean evil, but it also means worthless, ordinary, or of no account.

Life with Heaven in Mind. In John Bevere's amazing book *Driven by Eternity*, he challenges the body of Christ to live with the Bema Seat in mind. His point is that *where* you spend eternity is determined by what you do with the cross; *how* you spend eternity is determined by what you do after you've engaged the cross. It's frightening and exciting to consider that we'll be rewarded by God for the way we live out our lives in faith here on earth.

Another key thought Bevere presents in his book is the mathematical truth that any number divided by infinity will equal zero. This life, if we consider it in the context of eternity, is zero years long. The psalmist wrote that this life is but a breath (Psalm 144:4), passing like a blink in comparison to eternity. And we have that breath, that blink, that flash, to invest in an eternal reward.

Imagine you were approached by an investor and he offered you the chance to purchase a stock in a company the day before it went public. Let's say you were able to invest a thousand dollars at a penny per stock. That would be one hundred thousand shares. The next day, the stock opens worth ten dollars per stock. That means that in one day, on an investment of a thousand dollars, your stock would be worth a million dollars. You would have been made into a millionaire in a day.

My point is this: in light of eternity, where God is prepared to reward someone for giving another a cup of cold water, wouldn't it be worth considering the potential reward of a life lived in obedience to God, who will reward people with treasure that moth and rust will not corrupt?

If Jesus were to walk down the aisle of church this Sunday and say it was time for any one of us to come home to our reward, would we wish that we had given more, prayed more, worked less, cared for the hurting more, and obeyed more?

You need not be concerned about this doctrine leading you into a works-based mindset. This reward is measured by both action and motivation. God will not judge the works alone, but the motivation behind the works. Religion is interested in what you do, but intimacy wants to know why you did it. In the same way, this rewarding of the saints will have as much to do with our motivation as the quality of the good works themselves. That's the difference between what will be gold and what will be hay. Not what was done, but why it was done.

It will be both a wonderful and terrible day. Will the Lord value fame or humility, wealth or generosity, power or meekness? His Word has revealed what He values. Have we matched our actions and motivation with His Word?

This doctrine is considered an *elementary* doctrine, yet many of us live far from its truth. We must determine in our hearts to live with eternity in mind, to value things in light of their eternal weight, not their temporal gain.

Our North American perspective of discipleship has drifted far from the original plan. Let's return to the foundational principle of living with heaven in mind. If you're feeling the conviction of the Holy Spirit, pray the prayer below.

Father, I have allowed the concerns of this life to get in the way of hearing Your call to live with eternity in mind. I want my time before Jesus' judgement seat to be a time of rejoicing and worship, not regret. Lord,

I don't want to spend my season of investing in eternity on things that will have no bearing in eternity. Help me to see when You are setting me up to receive rewards in heaven. Help me to see beyond the moment and into forever. I repent for being so focused on earth and ask that You would teach me to be focused on heaven. In Jesus' mighty name, amen.

The Fear of the Lord. The foreboding you may be feeling right now is the fear of the Lord. It is the beginning of wisdom, the development of a greater concern for what offends heaven than for what offends man. The enemy tries to trick us into thinking it's bad because it doesn't feel good. Fearing the Lord means feeling deep responsibility and recognizing that you are not of this world.

Imagine what it would be like to be rewarded by heaven. Imagine us cheering for one another. Imagine receiving a crown of glory and laying it at Jesus' feet in an act of worship. Take an Olympics medals ceremony and multiply it by a hundred million, and you might come close to what this will be like. I can't wait.

But, as it is written, "What no eye has seen, nor ear heard, nor the heart of man imagined, what God has prepared for those who love him"...

—1 Corinthians 2:9

The White Throne Judgement

Then I saw a great white throne and him who was seated on it. From his presence earth and sky fled away, and no place was found for them. And I saw the dead, great and small, standing before the throne, and books were opened. Then another book was opened, which is the book of life. And the dead were judged by what was written in the books, according to what they had done. And the sea gave up the dead who were in it, Death and Hades gave up the dead who were in them, and they were judged, each one of them, according to what they had done. Then Death and Hades were thrown into the lake of fire. This is the second death, the lake of fire. And if anyone's name was not found written in the book of life, he was thrown into the lake of fire.

—Revelation 20:11–15 (emphasis added)

When Will it Happen? After the thousand-year reign of Jesus, Satan will be released for a season to deceive the nations. The Bible says that the number who are deceived will outnumber the sands of the sea. This may seem ridiculous. Why would God allow this, and why would anyone be deceived when Jesus is right there for all to see?

However, the issue isn't whether or not they see Jesus. In fact, the character of God is the reason the enemy will be released. Simply put, even though He will have ruled for a thousand years, justly and righteously for all to see, God will not arbitrarily force anyone to serve Him. This season will satisfy the love of God by allowing mankind the choice of serving Him.

Christ's capacity for freedom is amazing, and His willingness to face rejection on account of His integrity is staggering. It makes me love Him more.

What Will Happen? At the end of that season, all the remaining dead will rise. Every person great and small throughout history will stand before the Lord. What they have done will be read to them, and they will have no defence. If a name is not found in the book of life, they will be sent to the lake of fire—the second death, the final place of eternal torment.

The Judgement Seat of Christ is meant for believers in Jesus, whereas the White Throne Judgement is meant for the rest of humanity. One is for reward, the other for judgement.

Conclusion

Many in the body of Christ lack an understanding of the elementary doctrines of Jesus, and this results in a hunger that seems to never be satisfied. But with the foundational principles of the doctrine of Jesus clear, we can move forward to the next level of revelation and intimacy with

Jesus. Once we understand the elementary, we will be able to comprehend greater things.

> Therefore let us leave the elementary doctrine of Christ and go on to maturity, *not laying again a foundation of repentance from dead works and of faith toward God, and of instruction about washings, the laying on of hands, the resurrection of the dead, and eternal judgement.*
> —Hebrews 6:1–2 (emphasis added)

chapter seven

Transition

As we transition into the ancient pillars, I would like to take a moment to establish what they are as a whole. These ancient pillars that hold up an open heaven are structures of the mind—mindsets, predetermined positions of thought, that we establish so that we can experience the openness of heaven. They are what God designed to be the authentic forms of strongholds.

> *And David lived in the stronghold and called it the city of David. And David built the city all around from the Millo inward.*
>
> —2 Samuel 5:9

The Millo, or rampart, was a part of the fortifications in the city of Jerusalem, which means "teachings of peace." These pillars are, therefore, the strongholds of the teachings of peace. The Prince of Peace has provided strongholds that allow for us to engage the teachings of peace in our lives.

> You keep him in perfect peace whose mind is stayed on you, *because he trusts in you. Trust in the Lord forever, for the Lord God is an everlasting rock.*
>
> —Isaiah 26:3–4 (emphasis added)

*do not be anxious about anything, but in everything by prayer and sup-
plication with thanksgiving let your requests be made known to God.*
And the peace of God, which surpasses all understanding, will
guard your hearts and your minds *in Christ Jesus.*

—Philippians 4:6–7 (emphasis added)

God perfected in strongholds what the enemy counterfeited in
them. Whether a stronghold is godly or demonic depends on what it's
founded on—what is false or what is absolute. We're going to look at
stronghholds that are based on the ab-
solutes of God. Or said another way,
godly strongholds.

> Whether a stronghold is
> godly or demonic
> depends on what it's
> founded on—what is false
> or what is absolute.

In the next six chapters, we'll
examine the six ancient pillars, or
structures of thought, including what
they are and how they are connected
to the elementary doctrines. We'll
look at a resulting *renovated thought* for each pillar, which is an "I" statement declaring our renewed clarity of identity. As well, each pillar has a
glorified response, which is our lived-out expression of the revelation that
is given to us through the new stronghold of thought. Finally, there
will be a simple *prayer* to help us engage the new stronghold of thought,
which calls to mind the first elementary doctrine (repenting from dead
works), and then embrace the mindset of heaven. At the end of each
chapter, there will also be a *confession* which I encourage you to incorpo-
rate into your daily prayers.

The Power of Confession

Confession often gets a bad rap in the body of Christ because of excesses
that have existed in the past, such as prosperity doctrines, or name-it-and-
claim-it confessions. Sadly, out of fear we have thrown the baby out with
the bathwater and lost sight of this powerful element of our discipleship.

We need to understand three truths before we look at confession.
The first is that confession brings order to confusion.

In the beginning, God created the heavens and the earth. The earth was without form and void, *and darkness was over the face of the deep. And the Spirit of God was hovering over the face of the waters.*

And God said, *"Let there be light," and there was light. And God saw that the light was good. And God separated the light from the darkness.*

—Genesis 1:1–4 (emphasis added)

"Without form," in the original language, means a wasteland, but the word also means chaos and confusion. Our first introduction to earth is a formless wasteland of confusion and chaos, like a garbage dump with broken items strewn about.

My friend Allan Derry, who founded the Dream Centre in Medicine Hat and presently leads Church Unlimited in Vancouver, shared this second truth with me: God's kingdom is voice-activated.

And God said, *"Let there be light," and there was light. And God saw that the light was good. And God separated the light from the darkness.*

—Genesis 1:3–4 (emphasis added)

God spoke into that confusion and brought light to it, and in that speaking He brought order.

The third truth is that we are made in His image.

Then God said, "Let us make man in our image, *after our likeness. And let them have dominion over the fish of the sea and over the birds of the heavens and over the livestock and over all the earth and over every creeping thing that creeps on the earth."*

So God created man in his own image, *in the image of God he created him; male and female he created them.*

—Genesis 1:26–27 (emphasis added)

You and I are created in the image of the voice activator, and because of that we have the same speaking power that God has—not in a creative sense, but a confessing sense. We cannot speak something into existence, but we can agree with what heaven has already spoken over situations.

What Is Confession?

But what does it say? "The word is near you, in your mouth and in your heart" (that is, the word of faith that we proclaim); because, if you confess with your mouth that Jesus is Lord and believe in your heart that God raised him from the dead, you will be saved. For with the heart one believes and is justified, and with the mouth one confesses and is saved.

—Romans 10:8–10 (emphasis added)

The Greek word for confess is *homologeō*, a compound word from *homou*, which means "together," and *logos*, which means something that has been said. Confession means being together with what has been said—or said another way, agreeing with what has already been said.

With the heart we believe and are justified (made righteous), and through our spoken agreement with what has already been said about Jesus, we activate our salvation. Like God, we speak over our wasteland of confusion and confess the lordship of Jesus over it, bringing kingdom order to the confusion. God looks upon this and declares it good.

Death and life are in the power of the tongue, and those who love it will eat its fruits.

—Proverbs 18:21

The value of confession is in the fact that salvation, the most important miracle to mankind, is activated through confession. There is tremendous power in our words, but often we misunderstand how to use them for our benefit. We are not called to just speak out and expect results, but rather to have our confessions be the enforcement of what the Lord has already said.

Transition

Rule of Math

Study and be eager and do your utmost to present yourself to God approved (tested by trial), a workman who has no cause to be ashamed, correctly analyzing and accurately dividing [rightly handling and skillfully teaching] the Word of Truth.

—2 Timothy 2:15, AMPC (emphasis added)

I am not a mathematician by any stretch. However, we all understand that in addition and multiplication, the order of numbers is irrelevant. 2 + 1 = 3 and 1 + 2 = 3, and 2 x 3 = 6 and 3 x 2 = 6. The order of the numbers are very important, though, in division. 9 ÷ 3 = 3, but 3 ÷ 9 = 0.33.

My point is that Scripture tells us to rightly divide the word of truth. When we switch the order of confession from heaven to earth to earth to heaven, we get very different results. This subtle trick of the enemy has caused earthly agendas to pollute confessions, resulting in self-promoting confessions that don't line up with heaven's agenda.

Matthew 16 gives us a wonderful perspective of confession. When Jesus asks the disciples who men say He is, they offer their thoughts. Some say Elijah or John the Baptist. Jesus then asks them who they think He is, and Peter chimes in.

Simon Peter replied, "You are the Christ, the Son of the living God."

And Jesus answered him, "Blessed are you, Simon Bar-Jonah! For flesh and blood has not revealed this to you, but my Father who is in heaven. *And I tell you, you are Peter, and on this rock I will build my church, and the gates of hell shall not prevail against it. I will give you the keys of the kingdom of heaven, and whatever you bind on earth shall be bound in heaven, and whatever you loose on earth shall be loosed in heaven.*"

—Matthew 16:16–19 (emphasis added)

Sweet Peter (I can't wait to meet him) confesses Jesus as the Son of the living God. Jesus responds by blessing him and declaring that this was a confession from heaven to earth (*"For flesh and blood has not revealed this to you, but my Father who is in heaven."*)

Then Jesus goes on to say some extraordinary things. I'd like to look at the last two verses from the Amplified Bible:

> *And I tell you, you are* Peter [Greek, Petros—*a large piece of rock*], *and on* this rock [Greek, petra—*a huge rock like Gibraltar*] *I will build My church, and the gates of Hades (the powers of the infernal region) shall not overpower it [or be strong to its detriment or hold out against it].*
>
> *I will give you* the keys of the kingdom of heaven; *and whatever you bind (declare to be improper and unlawful) on earth* must be what is already bound in heaven; *and whatever you loose (declare lawful) on earth* must be what is already loosed in heaven.
>
> —Matthew 16:18–19, AMPC (emphasis added)

This is so important. First, Jesus renamed Simon (which means "heard") to Peter, or Petros (which means a large rock). But Jesus doesn't say that upon this Petros He will build His church, but upon this *petra* (rock). Why the difference? Jesus wasn't declaring that the church would be built upon a man but upon the man's confession. Peter is forever named in light of his confession, but the church is built on Jesus.

Confession is not founded in man, but in Jesus. Jesus hints at how it works in the following verse, by saying that He will give us the keys to the kingdom.

Keys open things that already exist. My wife Cathy is a real estate agent. The final step in the sale of a home is the release of the keys. When you get the keys, you own the home. Furthermore, a homebuilder releases the keys after the home is complete and ready to be moved into. You don't build a house with keys; you unlock it to live in it with keys. That's why Jesus said that whatever we bind or loose on earth must have already been bound or loosed in heaven.

When Adam and Eve fell into sin in the Garden of Eden, the kingdom order of earth was thrown into a chaotic, confused wasteland. Every person born from then on faced that same inner confusion. But as we, the redeemed whose lives have been returned to kingdom order through our confession of faith in the lordship of Jesus, come into agreement and confess what heaven has already said about any circumstance, we activate the stirring of kingdom order in the chaotic wasteland of the world around us.

Confession isn't coercion. When we confess what heaven has already said, we walk in agreement, not trying to get heaven to agree with us.

Sickness and disease have already been judged.

Pain has already been judged.

Sadness, tears, and depression have already been judged.

All the works of the devil have already been judged. Our confession needs to match that.

In the same way, heaven has declared who you are in Jesus.

Heaven has declared love for you.

Heaven has declared peace and joy for you.

Heaven has declared you righteous.

Confession is agreement with what heaven has already said, and in the context of the pillars, confession activates the promises of heaven over our thinking, releasing us to "reign in life," as Paul promised:

> *For if, because of one man's trespass, death reigned through that one man, much more will those who receive the abundance of grace and the free gift of righteousness* reign in life through the one man Jesus Christ.
> —Romans 5:17 (emphasis added)

So, what are the pillars? They are:

1. The old man is dead.
2. We are filled with God Himself.
3. We are children with an inheritance.
4. We are naturally supernatural.
5. All things are possible with God.
6. God is good.

Simple yet profound, these six pillars hold up an open heaven over us. Let's begin.

chapter eight

The Old Man is Dead

What shall we say then? Are we to continue in sin that grace may abound? By no means! How can we who died to sin still live in it? Do you not know that all of us who have been baptized into Christ Jesus were baptized into his death? *We were buried therefore with him by baptism into death, in order that, just as Christ was raised from the dead by the glory of the Father,* we too might walk in newness of life.

For if we have been united with him in a death like his, we shall certainly be united with him in a resurrection like his. We know that our old self was crucified with him in order that the body of sin might be brought to nothing, *so that we would no longer be enslaved to sin.* For one who has died has been set free from sin. *Now if we have died with Christ, we believe that we will also live with him. We know that Christ, being raised from the dead, will never die again; death no longer has dominion over him. For the death he died he died to sin, once for all, but the life he lives he lives to God. So you also* must consider yourselves dead to sin and alive to God in Christ Jesus.

—Romans 6:1–11 (emphasis added)

You Are a Terrible Sinner

I USED TO JOKE WHEN I PREACHED THAT I WAS GOOD AT SINNING. I WOULD tease my listeners, saying that sinning was the only thing I didn't need to practice, that it came quite naturally. We would all laugh a bit and then I would move on.

The problem is that I was teaching them something very wrong. I was teaching that they could not live free from sin, that they had to tolerate the fact that they were stuck between two conditions, holiness and sinfulness.

Statements like "I'm just a sinner saved by grace" and "That's just my old nature rising up again" are false. They point to a stronghold of thought that says salvation cleaned us but didn't cure us.

Nothing could be further from the truth.

Earlier in the book, I shared that salvation is not a reset button, but rather a return to our original design. Salvation made us new creations, fashioned in the image of God. I explained the symbolism of the body of sin and how baptism legally separates us from our old sin nature, the result of which is a new stronghold, an ancient pillar that will hold heaven open for you.

Your old man is dead. You're not good at sinning anymore because it's contrary to your new nature.

> ...to put off your old self, *which belongs to your former manner of life and is corrupt through deceitful desires, and to be* renewed in the spirit of your minds, and to put on the new self, created after the likeness of God *in true righteousness and holiness.*
> —Ephesians 4:22–24 (emphasis added)

You're a terrible sinner. You're no good at sinning at all. It's not natural for something in God's image to sin. Your new self is created after God's likeness in true righteousness and holiness. You no longer have a sin nature. It has been crucified and buried in the waters of baptism.

The old man is dead.

The Connection

If it isn't already obvious, the "old man is dead" pillar is founded in the doctrine of baptism. As the Apostle Paul clearly states, our old nature is crucified; it's buried and long gone. We are legally free from our old nature through baptism. However, we often don't live free.

Imagine you were in the market for a new home. You find a real estate agent and begin your search. You have criteria for the kind of home you need and a budget for what you can afford. So you approach a bank and secure a mortgage through a down-payment. All that's left to do is the house-hunting.

And then you find it: the perfect home for you. You love everything about it and you make an offer. The offer is accepted and all that's left is to sign off on the purchase. So you hire a solicitor to address all the legal matters on your behalf, and then he presents you with the documents that need your signature to complete the purchase.

The question is this: would you consider any homebuyer to be in their right mind if they spread out the legal documents and bill of sale in the solicitor's parking lot, sat down on them, and cried out, "Look at our beautiful new home"?

You would think they'd lost their mind.

Many Christians embrace the legality of their baptisms but don't live in their beautiful new home of freedom. Doctrine is like the rudder of a ship. It has the ability to steer you, but you don't worship the rudder; you use it to steer you to your destination. The doctrine of baptism should steer you to your new nature.

Sometimes we spend more time celebrating the doctrine than living in the promise available to us through the doctrine.

The phenomenal possibility for the Christian is this: you can live sin free.

Renovated Thought: I Am Free from Sin

I'm sure you've seen in movies or television a character, faced with a difficult choice, who sees a little angel and a little demon on their shoulders. The angel encourages them to do good and the demon tempts them to do bad. They are portrayed as the good and evil side of the person, both resident and fighting for their "host" to do their bidding.

Somehow Christians have considered this to be a real condition. Many of us believe that we've been liberated *from* sin but still live *in* sin. The little devil inside us has been revealed and now we need to fight him by ignoring him and doing what is right. But we all know that the devil inside will make us do bad stuff every once in a while. That's just the way it is. Sometimes we lose the fight because we want to do the bad thing, because the bad is still a part of us.

Many of us believe that we've been liberated *from* sin but still live *in* sin.

After all, isn't that what the Bible says? Paul even wrote about it, didn't he?

> *So I find it to be a law that* when I want to do right, evil lies close at hand. *For I delight in the law of God, in my inner being, but I see in my members another law waging war against the law of my mind and* making me captive to the law of sin that dwells in my members. *Wretched man that I am! Who will deliver me from this body of death?*
>
> —Romans 7:21–24 (emphasis added)

How do we reconcile what we read in Romans 6 and 8 with what we read in Romans 7? Sandwiched between these chapters of liberty is this troubling seventh chapter, which seems to contradict what is before and after it.

The key to understanding Romans 7 and its message is to answer three questions. Who was Paul writing to? How did he write to them? How did he close the thought?

First, Paul was writing to Jewish Romans.

> *Or do you not know,* brothers—for I am speaking to those who know the law—*that the law is binding on a person only as long as he lives?*
>
> —Romans 7:1 (emphasis added)

In the midst of bringing clarity to the Romans about freedom from sin and the death of the old man, Paul takes a moment to address any Jews who may hear his letter. He then goes on to write about life under the law and culminates with a discussion of a Jew's condition under the law.

But how he does this is important. When someone tells a story, a compelling way to share it is in first-person present tense. In short, this method of storytelling brings the listener or reader into the teller's emotions and difficulties. It creates an atmosphere of tension. Paul does this by sharing in present tense his past condition, so the Roman Jews can identify with their own tension in the law and see the value of faith in Jesus, which leads to the answer of the third question.

Look at how Paul relieves the tension through presenting Christ.

Wretched man that I am! Who will deliver me from this body of death? Thanks be to God through Jesus Christ our Lord! *So then, I myself serve the law of God with my mind, but with my flesh I serve the law of sin.*

There is therefore now no condemnation *for those who are in Christ Jesus. For the law of the* Spirit of life has set you free in Christ Jesus *from the law of sin and death.*

—Romans 7:24–8:2 (emphasis added)

Paul ends the thought by pointing his Jewish readers back to freedom in Christ, showing that through Jesus the law of the Spirit has set us free, and is greater than the law they previously served.

The Lie: You're a Sinner

The strength of this lie is in your capacity to sin. But the power found in the truth of this ancient pillar is that you no longer *have* to sin. You have victory over sin because of the work of the cross. Jesus made you new. You're a new creation and no longer subject to any yoke of slavery.

Up until now, you may have defined your freedom from sin through confession and repentance. This is absolutely true, but confession and repentance are still based on you being a slave to sin. A slave thinks that sin is an inevitability. You have capacity to sin because you're free to choose between sin and righteousness.

So what do I mean by the capacity to sin?

> A slave thinks that sin is an inevitability.

Freedom Is Your Ability to Choose

What then? Are we to sin because we are not under law but under grace? By no means! Do you not know that if you present yourselves to anyone as obedient slaves, you are slaves of the one whom you obey, either of sin, which leads to death, or of obedience, which leads to righteousness? But thanks be to God, that you who were once slaves of sin have become obedient from the heart to the standard of teaching to which you were committed, and, having been set free from sin, have become slaves of righteousness.

—Romans 6:15–18 (emphasis added)

Real freedom means you have the ability to choose. As a Christian, you have the choice whether to be a slave to sin or to righteousness. You are not forced into slavery. You don't have to be in bondage. Remember the checks and balances I discussed earlier? You have a free will. Your salvation and baptism free you from being bound to sin.

Remember the government of Christian? Let's look back at that analogy. Christian's minority government can only work if there's a coalition between the Spirit Party and the Soul Party. Prior to inviting the lordship of Christ into Christian's life, he lived under a dictatorship. He was enslaved to a dictator (Satan) through the alliance created through Adam called the old nature (see Romans 5:12). This dictator prohibited the Spirit Party from any form of influence in the governing of Christian. The constitution of the old nature—the passions of the flesh—held the Body Party captive with its desires for pleasure and leisure, igniting a craving for sin.

This is the condition of a person prior to accepting Jesus as Lord. Before we were saved, we suffered under the tyrannical dictatorship of

Satan. Under his rule, we were hopelessly bound to sin due to the alliance Adam made in the beginning, and the constitution requiring us to continue following its passions, which led us deeper and deeper into bondage.

One of my associates, Josh Frey, spoke recently made this brilliant statement. Craving comes from memory.

When the children of Israel were on their journey to the Promised Land, at one point they had been in the wilderness for some time. Some of them began to complain.

Now the rabble that was among them had a strong craving. And the people of Israel also wept again and said, "Oh that we had meat to eat! We remember the fish we ate in Egypt that cost nothing, the cucumbers, the melons, the leeks, the onions, and the garlic. But now our strength is dried up, and there is nothing at all but this manna to look at."
—Numbers 11:4–6

Your capacity to sin is found when your memory of sin creates a craving. Craving will cause you to remember the taste of sin, or its momentary pleasure—just like the rabble in Numbers 11 was craving the fish, meat, cucumbers, and so on. But all the while, they were forgetting that their craving had been satisfied in the slavery of Egypt!

Even more disturbing, in their desire to have the luxuries of slavery, they complained about God's provision for them. In their defence, I'm sure that if I had manna every day, I would long for a little variety.

The point of the manna is that the life of a disciple doesn't change. The cost of walking in righteousness is denying oneself and following the Lord. While it may not bring fame, wealth, influence, and worldly possessions, the narrow way is the way of life.

What You Feed Will Lead You

Our bodies reflect a spiritual truth. Diet and exercise have a massive impact on our physical health. If we live a lazy lifestyle with no activity, our bodies weaken and lose stamina. If we choose an unhealthy diet full of fats and sugars, we pay the price with excess weight that has a negative effect on our overall health.

The opposite is also true. If we choose to exercise and be active, our bodies remain strong and limber. If we eat healthily, our bodies flourish. However good exercise and nutritious food is for us, eating properly and exercising regularly is hard to establish. Sweating and running isn't all that fun, and chocolate tastes better than spinach.

But we know that after the body gets used to training and receiving proper nutrition, it begins to crave the good things rather than the bad. And when a proper diet is cheated on, the body responds by getting a little ill.

A spiritual truth is reflected in this: whatever you feed will lead you. If you feed your body poorly, it will crave bad things; if you let your fitness lag, you will prefer to watch TV rather than work out. Once you start eating proper food and exercising, the body desires those things as well. The same is true of the spirit. If you feed yourself from the menu of the passions of the flesh, your pull to those passions will be stronger than your pull to the things of the Spirit.

So if you want to weaken your pull to the passion of the flesh, you need to go on a diet. The only way to bring an end to a craving is to starve it. If a sin in your life consistently trips you up, you need to starve it to be free. As long as you answer the craving, in any form, you will feed the flesh the wrong things, strengthening your desire for the wrong things and weakening your strength to engage the things of the Spirit.

Remember that some temptations are location-specific. Don't stand in front of a chocolate cake when you're craving something sweet.

For when you were slaves of sin, you were free in regard to righteousness. But what fruit were you getting at that time from the things of which you are now ashamed? For the end of those things is death.
—Romans 6:20–21 (emphasis added)

Craving will always lead you to a dead end.

Glorified Response: Living a Sin-Free Life (Purity)

We have established that we *can* live sin-free, but how do we do it?

There Is Power in Weakness. We have a tendency to reduce the fruit of the Spirit to the limits of human strength, which sums up the spirit of religion's assignment on mankind: reduce them to the limits of their human strength and accuse them of not being good enough to have a relationship with God on account of their lack of strength.

But the fruit of the Spirit is love, joy, peace, patience, kindness, good-ness, faithfulness, gentleness, self-control; against such things there is no law. And those who belong to Christ Jesus have crucified the flesh with its passions and desires.

—Galatians 5:22–24

I have good news. The fruit of the Spirit comes from the Holy Spirit, not from you. They are meant to be supernatural boosters in your life that are so otherworldly that those around you will be struck by the goodness of God in you. When it comes to this pillar, we are given a powerful spiritual fruit to feast upon.

Self-Control. Here's the best part: self-control is not self-restraint. To assume that self-control is self-restraint is to suggest that there is some part of your old nature that's still alive and that you'll have to go to battle against it and subdue it, binding and imprisoning it again so you can remain righteous. That's simply not true. That old nature has been crucified with Christ through your baptism and it is gone!

Malcolm Smith wrote of this in his book, *The Power of the Blood Covenant.* He referred to the itch of the old nature like the itch on an amputated limb. Some people who have had a limb amputated suffer through phantom pain. While the pain is real, the limb where the pain is perceived is gone.

This is important. Many will say that the feeling associated with temptation isn't real. They're wrong; it is real, just like phantom pain is real—real but perceived to be in a location that no longer exists. It is located in memory. As I shared earlier, temptation depends on the cravings of memory.

One form of treatment for phantom pain is mirror therapy, where a mirror is used to reflect an image of the patient while getting physical therapy on the remainder of the limb. That way, the patient can see the therapy happen and observe that the limb is no longer there.

> *For those whom he foreknew he also predestined* to be conformed to the image of his Son, *in order that he might be the firstborn among many brothers.*
>
> —Romans 8:29 (emphasis added)

We are being conformed into the image of Jesus, meaning that we look like Him. Therefore, if I look into the reflection of the craving I feel, no matter how real it might seem, if it doesn't look like Jesus, then it isn't me.

Self-Control and Intimacy. The spirit of religion has robbed the body of Christ of true intimacy with God by perverting the fear of the Lord. The fear of the Lord is not meant to be something that drives us from Him, but rather something that makes us feel safe with Him.

> *Since we have these promises, beloved, let us cleanse ourselves from every defilement of body and spirit,* bringing holiness to completion in the fear of God.
>
> —2 Corinthians 7:1 (emphasis added)

The word Paul uses for fear is connected to the reverence one feels for a spouse. I live in perpetual awareness of my covenant with my wife Cathy. I revere her by living in a posture that honours our covenant. Cathy and I live every element of our lives with acute awareness of how we will affect each other. This is what the fear of the Lord exemplifies: a life lived in keen awareness of the covenant.

When I married Cathy, Single Landen died. I joyfully chose to no longer live for myself but for my wife. Single Landen no longer influences any decisions because Married Landen is the new Landen. If temptation were to come my way, there wouldn't be a fight between Married Landen and Single Landen about what to do, because my covenant with Cathy means that Single Landen no longer exists. It would be Married Landen making the choice to engage temptation, not some form of Single Landen returning to the scene.

Covenant, self-control, and intimacy work together on our behalf to produce purity.

My friend Darcy McAllister, the Personnel and Family Life Director for International Missions in the Pentecostal Assemblies of Canada, once told me that true intimacy occurs when a person has nothing to be ashamed of and nothing to protect. If I face anything that would cause a compromise in my covenant with Cathy, the first, safest, and most important place for me to go is to her. We are the covenant-keepers of our marriage.

Ultimately, our walk with Jesus is meant to be fearless and trusting. Having true intimacy with Jesus reflects that I have nothing to be ashamed of. Shame makes us hide. Religion depends on us thinking we have to hide things from Jesus, telling us that guilt and shame will be the best avenues for overcoming our shortfalls, that Jesus isn't safe, that He will be angry and upset.

What a lie from the pit of hell! Sweet Jesus is the safest place in the universe!

The word used in the Bible to describe self-control is a word that also describes continence, or the controlling of the bowels.

> You don't have real intimacy with Jesus if you only feel that you can connect with Him when you're doing well.

There are appropriate places to relieve the bowels and inappropriate places to relieve the bowels. Stay with me. In the context of our covenant, the most appropriate place to relieve ourselves is with Jesus. True intimacy with Jesus means being able to come to Him in the midst of phantom pain and say what is really happening. You don't have real intimacy with Jesus if you only feel that you can connect with Him when you're doing well. This is the essence of self-control. It is coming to Him and confessing your weakness so that He can empower you with His grace to strengthen you.

> *But he said to me,* "My grace is sufficient for you, for my power is made perfect in weakness." *Therefore I will boast all the more gladly of my weaknesses, so that the* power of Christ may rest upon me.
> —2 Corinthians 12:9 (emphasis added)

When we lean into the power of the covenant, we will never be left or forsaken by Jesus. We will be empowered by grace to live in purity.

Maybe you haven't had good experiences with intimacy. Perhaps people you've been in deep relationship with have failed you. Because of that, perhaps the word intimacy elicits fear in you.

Many people live outside of an important revelation, robbing them of the chance to establish a powerful relationship with God.

> God is not man, *that he should lie, or a son of man, that he should change his mind. Has he said, and will he not do it? Or has he spoken, and will he not fulfill it?*
> —Numbers 23:19 (emphasis added)

God is not some improved version of humanity, not even a version of super humanity. He is not a man; He is God, and He is good.

Intimacy means that you nothing to be ashamed of and nothing to protect. It's amazing to think that the creator of the universe desires to walk in intimate friendship with us.

Recently, a student in our discipleship school, Kristen, had an assignment to speak to the class. Kristen conveyed a perspective of God's love for us in a very unique way. She shared out of 1 John 4.

> *So we have come to know and to believe the love that God has for us. God is love, and whoever abides in love abides in God, and God abides in him. By this is love perfected with us, so that we may have confidence for the day of judgement, because as he is so also are we in this world.*

*There is no fear in love, but perfect love casts out fear. For fear has to
do with punishment, and whoever fears has not been perfected in love.*
—1 John 4:16–18

After she read the passage, she said that God is love and therefore
Jesus is love. Next, she replaced the word love with Jesus in the same
passage. And it came out like this:

*So we have come to know and to believe the Jesus that God has for us.
God is Jesus, and whoever abides in Jesus abides in God, and God abides
in him. By this is Jesus perfected with us, so that we may have confidence
for the day of judgement, because as he is so also are we in this world.
There is no fear in Jesus, but perfect Jesus casts out fear. For fear has to
do with punishment, and whoever fears has not been perfected in Jesus.*

Isn't that beautiful? Perfect Jesus casts out all fear. Fear not! There
is wonderful intimacy available to you should you choose to allow your
heart to be vulnerable and authentic.

The old man is dead. You are free from sin, and purity can help you
live sin-free.

The Choice Is Yours

Let not sin therefore reign in your mortal body, to make you
obey its passions. *Do not present your members to sin as instruments
for unrighteousness, but present yourselves to God as those who have
been brought from death to life, and your members to God as instruments for righteousness.* For sin will have no dominion over you,
since you are not under law but under grace.
—Romans 6:12–14 (emphasis added)

As Romans 6:12–14 explains, you have authority over sin. You are not
subject to the dictatorship of Satan. His dependence on the alliance of
the old nature has been broken by Christ, and through your acceptance

of the lordship of Jesus and making choice to be united with His death in baptism, you are free from your old nature. Sin does not have dominion over you... unless you choose to give it dominion.

And you are not alone. You have the Holy Spirit to aid you in overcoming sin:

> *Nevertheless, I tell you the truth:* it is to your advantage that I go *away, for if I do not go away, the Helper will not come to you. But if I go, I will send him to you. And when he comes, he will convict the world concerning sin and righteousness and judgement:* concerning sin, because they do not believe in me; concerning righteousness, because I go to the Father, and you will see me no longer; *concerning judgement, because the ruler of this world is judged.*
>
> —John 16:7–11 (emphasis added)

The Holy Spirit's role is in three major arenas: conviction of sin, righteousness, and judgement. To best understand this, we have to see who is under conviction and what conviction they're under.

Jesus carefully worded His description of the working of the Holy Spirit's conviction to give us clarity as to who is the focus of the conviction. The first conviction, sin, is directed toward the lost.

> *...concerning sin, because they do not believe in me...*
>
> —John 16:9

In this verse, Jesus is referring to the lost in the world, they who don't believe in Him. This means that the Holy Spirit will convict the world regarding the sin in their lives. His conviction will point out what separates the lost from God.

> *...concerning righteousness, because I go to the Father, and you will see me no longer...*
>
> —John 16:10

The conviction concerning righteousness is focused on disciples. When He says, "You will see me no longer," He is referring to His disciples and to us as believers in Him.

This is your help in purity. Our tendency is to ask if what we're doing is wrong. Is this movie wrong? Is this party wrong? Are these thoughts wrong? Because the old man is dead, you no longer have a natural tendency to do wrong; your tendency is to do right. So the Holy Spirit doesn't ask you if what you're doing is wrong. He will ask if what you are doing is right!

The Holy Spirit will convict you of the rightness of your actions. He will ask you, *Does what you're thinking, planning, or doing reflect the righteousness that has been purchased for you?* You get to choose.

Learning that sinning is a conscious choice helps us avoid it. The lie that sin will just happen is broken, but if it does happen it's because we choose for it to happen.

The old man is dead. You are free from the dominion of sin. If you choose to establish this structure of thought in your life, the good news is that you can live sin-free.

Pillar Prayer

Father, I have believed that sin still has dominion over me. I ask Your forgiveness for believing the lie that the cross didn't cure me. I repent of that mindset and choose to embrace the truth that my old nature is gone and not a part of me anymore. I receive the freedom of my new nature and I declare in Jesus name, "My old man is dead."

Thank You for my freedom. Strengthen my heart to not choose the passions of the flesh and engage the power of your Spirit.

Thank You for Your love for me, in Jesus' name, amen.

Pillar Confession

My old nature is dead. (Romans 6:11). I am united with Jesus in His death and resurrection through my confession of His lordship (Romans 10:9).

My baptism forever separated me from my old nature (Romans 6:6–7), and because of God's grace I can live sin-free today (Romans 6:14).

chapter nine

Filled with God Himself

Do you not know that you are God's temple and that God's Spirit dwells in you? *If anyone destroys God's temple, God will destroy him. For God's temple is holy, and you are that temple.*

Let no one deceive himself. If anyone among you thinks that he is wise in this age, let him become a fool that he may become wise. For the wisdom of this world is folly with God. *For it is written, "He catches the wise in their craftiness," and again,* "The Lord knows the thoughts of the wise, that they are futile." *So let no one boast in men. For all things are yours, whether Paul or Apollos or Cephas or the world or life or death or the present or the future—all are yours, and you are Christ's, and Christ is God's.*

—1 Corinthians 3:16–23 (emphasis added)

Weariness

I'VE GONE THROUGH LENGTHY SEASONS IN MINISTRY WHEN I GREW TIRED OF defending the Holy Spirit.

The charismatic movement, while not young, is still maturing. In the 90s, the outpourings of God's Spirit in Toronto, Pensacola, and Calgary, among others, defined for me what the charismatic movement looked like: vibrant worship, renewed passion for God and His presence, and this other phenomena—manifestations. People would "fall under the power." They would shake, laugh, yell, and sometimes scream or jerk. This brought about a conflict within the body of Christ that continues to bring tension between belief systems and brothers and sisters within the church. How could this be God? How does such disorderly activity point to the moving of the Holy Spirit?

I ran in headlong. The experience of His presence and power was, and still is, amazing. But in the midst of all that was good, there was much to attack. It seemed like critics in every service I stewarded. I spent hours and hours defending different manifestations—the length of worship, the way worship was expressed, the purpose of flags, dancing, shouting, and the like. Over and over, well-meaning people questioned, mean-spirited critics attacked, and I grew weary.

So I became a politician, making sure that the move of God was stewarded (boxed in). By most standards, my ministry would have still appeared charismatic, but I was cautious as to how far I permitted the Spirit to operate. I was grieving the Holy Spirit by allowing Him to only move to my level of comfort.

My ministry didn't reflect control or religiosity. There was liberty and growth, discipleship, and freedom. But I was afraid to allow things to go too far so I wouldn't have to defend it.

Then, one day, we were studying a book together as a staff. Normally I mark up books, underlining points, writing notes for later, etc. This book was no exception. It was really marked up… the sign of a good book for me. We went through one chapter per week as a staff and discussed how we felt about it.

We soon came to chapter on the importance of the Holy Spirit to the move of God, something that I, of course, would embrace and agree with. Yet I noticed that I had hardly made a mark in that chapter. When I realized it, the Lord spoke to me: "Your weariness in defending Me has led you to losing value of Me."

I was stunned. How this could be? I had always held a high value for the Lord in every aspect of my life.

His response was equally stunning. "As Father, yes. As Son, yes. But as the Holy Spirit, you have begun to reject Me."

That's when this pillar became real to me. The baptism of the Holy Spirit is more than speaking in tongues, more than manifestations, more than a feeling. It is to be filled with God Himself.

Four Baptisms and a Funeral

Baptism 1: A Proselyte. The study of Jewish history shows us that baptism didn't show up on the world scene with the emergence of John the Baptist. Baptism was a requirement for any Gentile who wanted to convert to Judaism.

There were three components to Jewish conversion. The first was circumcision, the second was baptism, and the third was a sacrifice. Men had to be circumcised, both men and women had to be baptized in what was called a *mikveh*, and both had to offer a sacrifice. The intent of the baptism was to remove the stain of being a Gentile. It was a ritualistic washing to qualify a person to enter into the chosen race. This was a baptism *into* the Jewish religion.

Baptism 2: Repentance. John the Baptist's baptism was a baptism of repentance. It was a baptism *out* of religion. When the Pharisees and Sadducees tried to participate in John's baptism, he had some pretty strong words for them:

> But when he saw many of the Pharisees and Sadducees coming to his baptism, he said to them, "You brood of vipers! Who warned you to flee from the wrath to come? Bear fruit in keeping with repentance. And do not presume to say to yourselves, 'We have Abraham as our father,' *for I tell you, God is able from these stones to raise up children for Abraham. Even now the axe is laid to the root of the trees. Every tree therefore that does not bear good fruit is cut down and thrown into the fire.*
>
> "I baptize you with water for repentance, *but he who is coming after me is mightier than I, whose sandals I am not worthy to carry.* He will baptize you with the Holy Spirit and fire. *His winnowing fork is in his hand, and he will clear his threshing floor and*

gather his wheat into the barn, but the chaff he will burn with un-quenchable fire."

—Matthew 3:9–12 (emphasis added)

He accused the Pharisees and Sadducees of coming to what they thought would be just another religious cleansing to remove one's sin without intending to change. His challenge for them to bear the fruit of repentance shows his discernment of their hearts. They were doing what religion always does: holding a form of godliness but denying the power (see 2 Timothy 3:3). He was saying to them, "Show us the fruit of the repentance that you claim."

We could use the same message to challenges those of us in charismatic movement today.

There are a few interesting clues as to the purpose of John's baptism. He was sent to make a way for the Messiah, to make the crooked paths straight. Religion had become a crooked path for the children of Israel. John's baptism of repentance pointed not to *a* sacrifice, but to *the* sacrifice in Jesus the Messiah. The Jews were offended to be told they needed baptism. Their birth gave them the security of belonging to the chosen race. Yes, there were those who were able to become Jews by being proselytes, but those who claimed Abraham's promise by birth thought they had no need of repentance. John's message to Israel was to repent and turn away from the systems of men and embrace the promise of God.

John wasn't about to let leaders of a system get in the way of the Messiah. The separatist (Pharisee) and the righteous (Sadducee) works of men were no longer necessary or of any value. True repentance was to be shown through the circumcised heart by the baptism of the Holy Spirit. Because of the Messiah's perfect sacrifice, God worked on man's behalf; men no longer working for God's favour. God showed His love, kindness, and desire for relationship with man through the work of Jesus, our Saviour.

But even then, John made it clear that he was not the Messiah and that the baptisms of the Messiah would be even greater than the baptism of repentance.

Next, let's look at the fourth baptism before the third.

Baptism 4: A Funeral. John declared that Jesus would come to baptize in the Holy Spirit and fire. As we will see, baptism in the Holy Spirit is a baptism into power (Acts 1:8), but the baptism of fire is a baptism of judgement (1 Corinthians 3:13, Revelation 20:14–15). The baptism of the Holy Spirit is meant to be experienced on this side of eternity; the baptism of fire will be experienced on the other side. John again shows us the difference in his encounter with the Pharisees and Sadducees.

> *Even now the axe is laid to the root of the trees. Every tree therefore that does* not bear good fruit is cut down and thrown into the fire… *His winnowing fork is in his hand, and he will clear his threshing floor and* gather his wheat into the barn, but the chaff he will burn with unquenchable fire.
>
> —Matthew 3:10, 12 (emphasis added)

I find it interesting that John only focuses on explaining fire. He chooses to let Jesus teach us about the baptism of the Holy Spirit. Why? Just like you and me, John could only release the revelation that he possessed.

There are two judgements of fire. Earlier I wrote that believers' works will be judged by fire for the sake of a reward. There is no need for us to panic or be afraid for our salvation. However, the second immersion in fire is something to be truly feared. He will gather His wheat and throw the chaff into an unquenchable fire.

> *Then I saw a great white throne and him who was seated on it. From his presence earth and sky fled away, and no place was found for them. And I saw the dead, great and small, standing before the throne, and books were opened. Then another book was opened, which is the book of life. And the dead were judged by what was written in the books, according to what they had done. And the sea gave up the dead who were in it, Death and Hades gave up the dead who were in them, and they were judged, each one of them, according to what they had done. Then Death and Hades were thrown into the lake of fire. This is the second*

*death, the lake of fire. And if anyone's name was not found written in
the book of life, he was thrown into the lake of fire.*

—Revelation 20:14–15

*But as for the cowardly, the faithless, the detestable, as for murderers,
the sexually immoral, sorcerers, idolaters, and all liars,* their portion
will be in the lake that burns with fire and sulfur, which is the
second death.

—Revelation 21:8 (emphasis added)

The gathering of the wheat is the gathering of those who have chosen faith in Christ. They will be gathered into His safekeeping. The chaff,
however, will not. The baptism of fire is the consequence of not choosing Jesus. It is death, the final place of eternal torment for rejecting Jesus.

For a moment, let that word sink in: *eternal.* Sometimes in our own
self-absorbed thoughts, we forget that eternity has two destinations—
His presence or torment—as the result of what we do with the cross
of Jesus. May that be a motivator in our evangelistic perspective. The
eternal baptism will be a funeral, the final separation of life from death.

Fire, Repentance, and Rest. Are there present-day applications
for the baptism of fire? The good news is yes.

For the Lord your God is a consuming fire, a jealous God.

—Deuteronomy 4:24

Recently while meditating on the fire of God, the Holy Spirit reminded me of this passage, that He is a consuming fire.

The tabernacle of Moses' day and the temple that Solomon built
were both meant to be types of the new covenant believer's life. We
are meant to have the altar of sacrifice active in our lives through confession and repentance. We are meant to have a soul connection with
God through intercession, worship, and the Word of God, symbolized
through the candle stand, the showbread, and altar of incense. We are also
meant to have a one-on-one, holy-of-holies intimate relationship with
His very presence, and to be carriers of that presence wherever we go.

111

He brought my focus to the altar of sacrifice. In our lives, the altar of sacrifice is represented in our acts of confession and repentance. Jesus, our ultimate sacrifice, completed the work of eradicating our sin condition and bondage on the cross, releasing us to walk in authority over sin and break its authority over ourselves through confession and repentance.

But how does this relate to a baptism of fire?

When the tabernacle and temple were dedicated, God performed a sign of His favour by consuming the sacrifices on the altar with fire that came out from the holy of holies.

And fire came out from before the Lord and consumed the burnt offering and the pieces of fat on the altar, and when all the people saw it, they shouted and fell on their faces.

—Leviticus 9:24

As soon as Solomon finished his prayer, fire came down from heaven and consumed the burnt offering and the sacrifices, and the glory of the Lord filled the temple.

—2 Chronicles 7:1

You and I, now living in the favour of the New Covenant, have access to this same consuming fire.

Fire and Transformation. Throughout the book, I have championed participating in the renovation of our minds, yet we can't ignore the fact that God will on occasion miraculously change a person's heart. With no apparent process, drug addicts are delivered, alcoholics are set free, the oppression of depression is lifted, and the gossiper gains control of their tongue, among many other examples.

In scripture, we see that people are amazed at such transformations. Consider the demon-possessed man from the Gadarenes:

And he went away and began to proclaim in the Decapolis how much Jesus had done for him, and everyone marveled.

—Mark 5:20

And notice Zacchaeus' transformation:

And Zacchaeus stood and said to the Lord, "Behold, Lord, the half of my goods I give to the poor. And if I have defrauded anyone of anything, I restore it fourfold."

—Luke 19:8

Paul's conversion was hard to believe for many as well:

And when he had come to Jerusalem, he attempted to join the disciples. And they were all afraid of him, for they did not believe that he was a disciple. But Barnabas took him and brought him to the apostles and declared to them how on the road he had seen the Lord, who spoke to him, and how at Damascus he had preached boldly in the name of Jesus.

—Acts 9:26–27

I believe that the repentance of a sincere lover of Jesus can invite the miraculous fire of God to consume not just the sin but the issue behind the sin on the altar of confession. Look at this passage, from when Isaiah was confronted with his sin:

And I said: "Woe is me! For I am lost; for I am a man of unclean lips, and I dwell in the midst of a people of unclean lips; for my eyes have seen the King, the Lord of hosts!"
Then one of the seraphim flew to me, having in his hand a burning coal that he had taken with tongs from the altar. And he touched my mouth and said: "Behold, this has touched your lips; your guilt is taken away, and your sin atoned for."

—Isaiah 6:5–7

Whether it's through a process of renovation or a miraculous consuming fire, we have access to the fire of God to burn up that which robs us of intimacy with Him. When we have a profound sense of sorrow for any stronghold that's stealing kingdom fullness from us, we have the freedom to invite the fire of God to consume it.

We can do this from rest because it's a miraculous manifestation, not something we earn, and it is meant to ignite hope.

Many live with an overwhelming sense of hopelessness regarding their areas of perceived weakness. All of us at one time or another have felt like we don't have the strength to overcome, so we end up living in a way that makes us feel dysfunctional, tolerating weakness and returning over and over to the sin and feeling like we can never be free. When we're in that place, we can invite the fire of God to burn it up.

But what if it doesn't get burned up? Let hope arise! If we don't experience a miraculous breakthrough, that means God is with us and we have the power to overcome! It means that your weakness isn't as strong as you think, and He wants you to participate in the victory over it. Either way, we win!

Baptism 3: The Holy Spirit. Jesus did everything on purpose. When He was baptized, He chose the Jordan. The reason is that different kinds of baptismal water had different value. In fact, there were six descending orders of ritualistic immersion in the Jewish culture. The highest was flowing water or a spring. It was called living water. To fulfill all righteousness, Jesus had to be baptized in living water. Does that phrase sound familiar?

> *The Samaritan woman said to him, "How is it that you, a Jew, ask for a drink from me, a woman of Samaria?" (For Jews have no dealings with Samaritans.)*
>
> *Jesus answered her,* "If you knew the gift of God, and who it is that is saying to you, 'Give me a drink,' you would have asked him, and he would have given you living water."
>
> *The woman said to him, "Sir, you have nothing to draw water with, and the well is deep. Where do you get that living water? Are you greater than our father Jacob? He gave us the well and drank from it himself, as did his sons and his livestock."*
>
> *Jesus said to her, "Everyone who drinks of this water will be thirsty again, but whoever drinks of the water that I will give him will never be thirsty again. The water that I will give*

him will become in him a spring of water welling up to eternal life."

—John 4:9–14 (emphasis added)

Whoever believes in me, as the Scripture has said, "Out of his heart will flow rivers of living water."' Now this he said about the Spirit, whom those who believed in him were to receive, *for as yet the Spirit had not been given, because Jesus was not yet glorified.*

—John 7:38–39 (emphasis added)

The baptism Jesus promised was a baptism into life—the Holy Spirit filling you with living water; being filled with God Himself. Ponder that.

We say that we ask Jesus into our hearts, and that's a nice statement. But salvation comes from believing in the work of the cross, confessing Jesus' lordship, and living submitted to His lordship. Believing in Him and being filled with Him are two different things. Our salvation comes upon confessing Jesus, but our baptism is our legal separation from our old man and the public declaration of our intention to serve Jesus. He is not just in our hearts; we must choose Him to be Lord over our hearts.

The Connection

This pillar is connected to the elementary doctrine of repentance from dead works.

It is the Spirit who gives life; the flesh is no help at all. *The words that I have spoken to you are spirit and life.*

—John 6:63 (emphasis added)

Such is the confidence that we have through Christ toward God. Not that we are sufficient in ourselves *to claim anything as coming from us, but our sufficiency is from God, who has made us sufficient* to be ministers of a new covenant, not of the letter but of the Spirit. For the letter kills, but the Spirit gives life.

Now if the ministry of death, carved in letters on stone, *came with such glory that the Israelites could not gaze at Moses' face because of its glory, which was being brought to an end,* will not the ministry of the Spirit have even more glory? *For if there was glory in the ministry of condemnation, the ministry of righteousness must far exceed it in glory.*

—2 Corinthians 3:4–9 (emphasis added)

As I wrote earlier, John's was a baptism of repentance, bringing people out of religion and preparing them for the coming Messiah. Life that's filled with the Spirit is anything but dead works. It means living with true repentance (changing one's mind) from trying to please God with religious activity. It means living a life that represents a kingdom that is not made of words but power (1 Corinthians 4:20). The Old Covenant words no longer represent the nature of God's kingdom. Jesus came to fulfill the Old Covenant and establish a new covenant sealed in the gift of the Holy Spirit.

And it is God who establishes us with you in Christ, *and has anointed us, and who has also put his seal on us and* given us his Spirit in our hearts as a guarantee.

—2 Corinthians 1:21–22 (emphasis added)

Guarantee is translated from the Greek word *arrhabon,* which is the same as a down-payment. In other words, the Spirit is given to us like a down-payment for the rest of what God has for us.

Think of it this way. God has given us Jesus to set us free from powerless formality, a condition in which we were far away, and brought us near to Him in relationship (Ephesians 2:13). God established us in Christ, making us new (2 Corinthians 5:17). He then guaranteed heaven's abundance for us by filling us with Himself via the Holy Spirit.

But what does this mean?

Filled with God Himself

Renovated Thought: I Lack Nothing

And God is able to make all grace abound to you, so that having all suf-
ficiency in all things at all times, you may abound in every good work.
—2 Corinthians 9:8

This verse is often, and correctly, used in its context in the realm of giving. However, the verse doesn't limit itself to finances. *"Having all sufficiency in all things at all times"* sounds to me like it concerns more than money.

Here's the point. You are filled with God Himself. You are filled with the Author of all. When filled with the Holy Spirit, you not only lack nothing, it is *impossible* for you to be in lack. The promise is all sufficiency in all things at all times. All means all.

> When filled with the Holy Spirit, you not only lack nothing, it is *impossible* for you to be in lack.

Think of it this way. Most of us have mortgages on our homes. To obtain a mortgage, you need a down-payment. Different regions have different laws, but for the sake of an example, let's say you need five percent of the borrowed amount to secure the loan. If you want a home that's priced at $400,000, you'll have to provide a $20,000 down-payment. You give the bank your $20,000, and in return they give you the other $380,000. You are then indebted to the bank until the mortgage and interest are paid back.

Being filled with God Himself avails you of the abundance of heaven. This pillar opens you to heaven's abundance because the Spirit is given to you as a down-payment. All the kingdom's resources are made available to you because of the down-payment of the Spirit.

But we are not debtors. Jesus paid our debt to God. Our sin has been addressed through the blood of Christ. We cannot be held in debt to God.

Let's go back to the mortgage metaphor. You would look pretty silly if you came to the seller of the home with only your down-payment in hand. You would be $380 000 short.

117

Amazingly, the down-payment of the Holy Spirit is the fullness of the abundance of heaven. The Holy Spirit is not a portion of heaven's bounty; He *is* heaven's bounty. He is all. In guaranteeing His claim to you, God pledged all of the resources of heaven by filling you with Holy Spirit, forever protecting you from being indebted. The fullness of God is released to you through the Holy Spirit. He is God and He resides in you.

Religion loves debt. The religious spirit loves for us to feel like we're indebted to God and have to try to pay Him back by lifeless activities. But God doesn't want debtors; He wants disciples. He doesn't lend to us; He gives to us. His abundance towards you is not OAC (on approval of credit). We don't receive from God on our religious credentials, but on the work of Christ. God is not some sort of knuckle-dragging loan collector waiting for you to make a mistake so He can come collecting for your mistakes. Jesus completely freed us of the debt of sin and our Father is not a loan shark.

Therefore, if you are established in Christ and ask for your free gift of the Holy Spirit, you have all of heaven's resources available to you. You lack *nothing.*

Glorified Response: Dwelling with God (Salvation)

How can we be filled with God Himself? Through salvation.

However, Jesus knew salvation wouldn't be enough to establish the kingdom of heaven through man. Would it be enough to eradicate sin? Yes. Would it be enough to ensure heaven for mankind? Yes. But it would not be enough to ensure that we live victorious, anointed, miracle filled lives. That would require living water, being filled with the Holy Spirit.

If salvation were enough, Jesus would have sent His disciples out immediately. But according to Luke, He didn't.

Thus it is written, that the Christ should suffer and on the third day rise from the dead, and that repentance for the forgiveness of sins should be proclaimed in his name to all nations, *beginning from Jerusalem. You are witnesses of these things.* And behold, I am sending the promise of my Father upon you. But stay in the city until you are clothed with power from on high.

—Luke 24:46–49 (emphasis added)

This pillar became real to me when I realized the value Jesus put on the Spirit in this verse. He was saying to His disciples, "I have done what I came to do for your salvation. Now wait until the Spirit has come to do what He is prepared to do: fill you with power."

Our salvation has brought us to a place where we are able to receive the *gift* of the Holy Spirit.

And Peter said to them, "Repent and be baptized every one of you in the name of Jesus Christ for the forgiveness of your sins, and you will receive the gift of the Holy Spirit."

—Acts 2:38 (emphasis added)

Picture it this way. In our home, whenever a guest stays with us, Cathy rallies our family to prepare our home to look its best. I get the vacuuming (which is great because I'm not crazy about the bathrooms). Off we scurry in a tornado of activity to get our chores done so that our home is in hosting condition. As is often the case, when guests arrive, they comment on how peaceful and clean our place is, not knowing the whirlwind it took to get it that way!

Our salvation prepares our hearts to host the Holy Spirit—not as a guest, but as a resident.

Do you not know that you are God's temple and that God's Spirit dwells in you?

—1 Corinthians 3:16

God's initial design was to go beyond salvation and make us each a place of His own habitation. He wants to dwell *in* you. That word, *dwell*, means to cohabit. The Holy Spirit is therefore a roommate. What a thought!

Tension in the Temple

Have you ever experienced tension with a person you are cohabiting with? Whether it's a roommate or spouse, tension has a way of causing separation even though you're in the same location.

When guests come to our home, we are on our best behaviour—not only to our guests, but to each other. I call it forced harmony, where "the look" is used to keep my behaviour in check and to make sure I don't say something to embarrass my spouse or parents (both of which I'm guilty of). As if somehow we're making the case that we're always this perfect.

We come down to breakfast freshly showered and made up, like we were prepared to go out to dinner... like it's always that way. We talk with one another sweetly, laughing off anything that would upset any normal person... like it's always that way. We quickly clean up messes and maintain a perfect home... like it's always that way. Oh, and our children obey us... like it's always that way.

In short, we perform for our guests, not showing them our real selves but a believable facsimile, hoping they believe the performance.

And we are exhausted when they finally leave.

The Holy Spirit isn't interested in being a guest. He wants to live in you. He wants to cohabit with you. But tension in your temple comes when you grieve Him.

And do not grieve the Holy Spirit of God, by whom you were sealed for the day of redemption.

—Ephesians 4:30

When we compartmentalize our lives, we live one way in one environment and another in a different one. Or, said another way, we live as hypocrites. This "guest" mentality allows us to be believable Christians at church but something far different at a jobsite.

Such hypocrisy creates tension with your roommate, the Holy Spirit. This inconsistency grieves Him and creates distance between you, leading to diminished intimacy and anointing, and carnality that looks to satiate hunger through the cravings of your former life and the passions of the flesh. It causes the very light of your witness to the world to be dimmed because the source of its power is restricted.

In short, the grief of the Holy Spirit will turn a river into a trickle.

Trickle from a River

When Jesus spoke of rivers of living water, He was referring to the Holy Spirit coming out of us. The way this happens is through the gifts and fruit of the Spirit. The Greek word Jesus used to describe the river is *potamos*, meaning floods and torrents. Jesus wasn't just speaking of a quiet river but of floodwaters, torrents, and explosions. When we grieve the Holy Spirit, those explosions turn into trickles of living water. A trickle doesn't have the same impact as a torrent. Neither will a believer who has reduced the Holy Spirit to an aggravating roommate.

You cannot have intimacy with Jesus and not with the Holy Spirit. They are one. You cannot have intimacy with the Father and not the Holy Spirit. You cannot have intimacy with Jesus and not with the Father. They are One. While each is separate and individual, they are one and inseparable. It is a mystery and it is all or nothing.

These torrents, these floodwaters, come from one source. When Paul was describing the gifts of the Spirit to the church in Corinth, he identified the Spirit as the source of it all.

> *All these are* empowered by one and the same Spirit, *who apportions to each one individually as he wills.*
> —1 Corinthians 12:11 (emphasis added)

When we grieve the Holy Spirit, we restrict the flow of living water coming out of us. The supernatural nature that is supposed to be alive in one who is filled with God Himself becomes limited because the outflow of God's life-giving nature is directly proportional to one's unhindered connection of the source.

Like a fire hydrant that's not connected to the water pipe, so is a believer who has not addressed the grief of the Holy Spirit.

Because we have the infamous blaspheming of the Spirit verse (Mark 3:29), we tend to think that the Holy Spirit must be a weaker part of the Trinity. Sort of like Jesus warning us not to bully the Holy Spirit or else He (Jesus) will come and bring the hammer down.

This isn't the case at all.

While the Trinity is, and will continue to be, a mystery, we get glimpses in Scripture of the binding properties of the Father, Son, and Holy Spirit. We know that love is the major binding component of the Trinity, but Jesus shows, through His response to both the Father and the Spirit, that honour is also present.

Jesus shows us His honour for the Father and His place of authority in the Trinity through His stewardship of the Father's will in Gethsemane. When Jesus spoke of His actions on earth:

> *So Jesus said to them, "Truly, truly, I say to you,* the Son can do nothing of his own accord, but only what he sees the Father doing. *For whatever the Father does, that the Son does likewise. For the Father loves the Son and shows him all that he himself is doing. And greater works than these will he show him, so that you may marvel."*
> —John 5:19–20 (emphasis added)

And look at the Father's response:

> *For the Father judges no one, but has given all judgement to the Son, that* all may honor the Son, just as they honor the Father. *Whoever does not honor the Son does not honor the Father who sent him.*
> —John 5:22–23 (emphasis added)

The Spirit likewise relates to us in the same manner:

> *When the Spirit of truth comes, he will guide you into all the truth,* for he will not speak on his own authority, but whatever he hears

he will speak, *and he will declare to you the things that are to come.*
He will glorify me, *for he will take what is mine and declare it to you.*
—John 16:13–14 (emphasis added)

That's why Jesus shows honour to the Holy Spirit by not tolerating the spirit of antichrist.

Foolish Declarations

Remember when King Saul made a foolish declaration? In 2 Samuel 14, Jonathan and his armour bearer start a battle with the Philistines, and the Lord joined the fray by giving Israel a victory. Saul, in his usual prideful way, declared that even though they had just won a battle, he wanted the people to fast until *"I am avenged on my enemies"* (1 Samuel 14:24).

Jonathan hadn't heard Saul's order and ate some wild honey. When the people warned him of the order, he lamented of his father's mistake, saying that because they were prohibited from eating, they were tired and would have a smaller victory than if they'd had the freedom to eat and gain strength. Israel went into battle anyway and won, but the people were so hungry that they fell upon the spoil, butchering animals and eating them raw, which was sinful.

Saul let pride get in his way in his rash declaration, leading his people into sin. On top of that, he was prepared to kill his son for breaking the vow. If it weren't for the people interceding on Jonathan's behalf, Saul's pride would have led him to kill his son, whose bravery hours before initiated the miraculous victory. Yet the Israelites were victorious.

But it doesn't sound like a victory, does it?

Saul's foolish declaration is much like foolish declarations by leaders today with regard to the moving of the Holy Spirit. By not discerning spirits, they risk leading their followers into judging others in the body of Christ, and worse yet risk, killing the destinies of sons and daughters under their leadership by questioning the source of their anointing. Their lack of honour toward the Spirit reflects the same condition in the leaders that Jesus faced in His day.

Jesus' honour of the Spirit's role is seen in His explanation of the unpardonable sin:

> *"Truly, I say to you, all sins will be forgiven the children of man, and whatever blasphemies they utter, but whoever blasphemes against the Holy Spirit never has forgiveness, but is guilty of an eternal sin"*—for they were saying, "He has an unclean spirit."
>
> —Mark 3:28–30 (emphasis added)

The accusation of the scribes was that Jesus was performing miracles through the powers of Satan. They were making the foolish declaration that Jesus was demon-possessed. Those accusations were unforgivable. Declaring the works of the Spirit as the works of the devil is not tolerated. Jesus, I believe, was declaring war against the first spirit to raise its head against Him: the spirit of antichrist.

Not Mr. Christ

We have a tendency to address Jesus Christ as if that were His first and last name. People didn't go around calling Him Mr. Christ. Christ is an adjective of Jesus. It describes what He is. He is the Messiah. He is anointed.

In the Greek, the word *Christos* means

> *...anointed, i.e. the Messiah, an epithet of Jesus... Christ was the Messiah, the Son of God anointed.*[6]

In his book, *When Heaven Invades Earth*, Bill Johnson notes that the world doesn't have a problem with Jesus. It is when He is Jesus Christ that the world has a problem with Him.[7]

---

6 Olive Tree Enhanced Strong's Dictionary, computer software, version 2011, Olive Tree Bible Software, accessed November 3, 2016 (www.olivetree.com).

7 Bill Johnson, *When Heaven Invades Earth* (Shippensburg, PA: Destiny Image, 2013).

When Jesus came down from His fast, the Bible says that He was filled with power from the Holy Spirit (Luke 4:14). He then went to the synagogue and read from Isaiah 61:

> *The Spirit of the Lord is upon me, because he has anointed me to proclaim good news to the poor.*
>
> —Luke 4:18

Jesus was fine in Nazareth before this. In this moment, however, He transforms from Jesus the son of Joseph to Jesus the Anointed One. They marvelled at Him in one moment and wanted to kill Him in the next.

What's my point? In his book, Johnson unveiled a truth that has helped me understand what prohibited me from walking in this pillar of an open heaven.

Understanding the Spirit of Antichrist

> *Beloved,* do not believe every spirit, but test the spirits *to see whether they are from God, for many false prophets have gone out into the world.* By this you know the Spirit of God: every spirit that confesses that Jesus Christ has come in the flesh is from God, *and every spirit that does* not confess Jesus is not from God. *This is* the spirit of the antichrist, *which you heard was coming and now is in the world already.*
>
> —1 John 4:1–3 (emphasis added)

According to Johnson, in the same way that we have made the mistake of thinking of Jesus Christ as a proper name, we have also made the mistake of relegating the meaning of antichrist to the man of lawlessness in the end times. While we are correct in that one definition, we overlook that 1 John 4 describes antichrist as a spirit.

"Anti" means against. "Christ" means anointed. Therefore, "antichrist" means against the anointing.

Up until Jesus was filled with power, He was not a threat. He had laid down His divinity for the purpose of redeeming mankind as an anointed man. He modelled for us what a life baptized in the Holy Spirit looks like, empowering us to be able to bring heaven to earth. Until Jesus was filled with power, He wasn't hated. How could His hometown spring into such a frenzy of hatred towards Him? Easy. They agreed with the spirit of antichrist. That spirit always says *no* to the anointing.

The Anointing Breaks the Yoke

And it shall come to pass in that day, that his burden shall be taken away from off thy shoulder, and his yoke from off thy neck, and the yoke shall be destroyed because of the anointing.

—Isaiah 10:27, KJV

I propose to you that the spirit of religion and the spirit of antichrist feed off of each other. Religion's yoke of performance and powerless activities is threatened by the power of the anointing. Antichrist works almost like a bodyguard for religion.

But it is the anointing that breaks the yoke.

Jesus' role was to bring salvation, while the Holy Spirit's role is to bring the anointing. It stands to reason then that the spirit of religion is okay with a powerless Jesus. But as soon as Jesus was filled with power, the bully had to rise up because religion was being threatened.

Antichrist's assignment is against the anointing. Jesus declared that the anointing came from the Holy Spirit. The Spirit anoints us. The Spirit's anointing is the power we need to be His witnesses. And it is the spirit of antichrist that manifests itself when we criticize and judge people who are anointed or are experiencing the anointing of the Holy Spirit.

It is dangerous to do so.

What Does the Anointing Look Like?

Abide in me, and I in you. As the branch cannot bear fruit by itself, unless it abides in the vine, neither can you, unless you abide in me. I

am the vine; you are the branches. Whoever abides in me and I in him,
he it is that bears much fruit, *for apart from me you can do nothing.*
—John 15:4–5 (emphasis added)

The anointing looks like fruit. While the manifestations discussed earlier point to the touch of God, bearing fruit points to being transformed by the power of God. Whether it's in personal transformation or in the working of the gifts of the Spirit, we must bear fruit.

In my journey of being weary to defend the move of the Spirit, I lacked clarity on how to steward altar calls when manifestations happened. However, I no longer judge the intensity of the touch of God on someone by how intense their manifestation may be; I judge it by the fruit of their lives.

In the body of Christ, the dysfunction of agreeing with the spirit of antichrist is a reality. However, the same immaturity exists in the charismatic arena.

Manifestation does not measure anointing; fruit does. We wouldn't receive someone's ministry as a healer if they shook when they prayed. We would receive them on account of the healing proof of their ministry.

We mustn't gauge the presence of God by the intensity of manifestations, nor should we expect each person to manifest in the same way (or at all). Rather, we need to champion fruit-bearing. We need to champion transformation. We need to champion His kingdom coming to earth.

> To reduce the transformation of our lives to a charismatic party is to miss the mission of the gospel.

The danger in the charismatic movement is that it can become about just having another "drunk in the Spirit" service. Playing with the power of the gospel becomes more important than using the power for the salvation of the world. To reduce the transformation of our lives to a charismatic party is to miss the mission of the gospel. Our transformation happens so we can bring the supernatural, miraculous power of God to our world, so that the world will see the will of God being proven here on Earth (Romans 12:2), and that His nature and love for the lost will be shown through us (Romans 5:8).

While I value the fact that a manifestation of the Spirit points to the potential of an individual's transformation, just like a running engine can point to the *potential* of a vehicle's horsepower, that manifestation does nothing to prove the condition of the individual, much like a running engine doesn't guarantee potential horsepower. Only through fruit can you tell whether the manifestation confirms transformation.

> You will recognize them by their fruits. *Are grapes gathered from thornbushes, or figs from thistles? So, every healthy tree bears good fruit, but the diseased tree bears bad fruit.* A healthy tree cannot bear bad fruit, nor can a diseased tree bear good fruit. *Every tree that does not bear good fruit is cut down and thrown into the fire.* Thus you will recognize them by their fruits.
>
> —Matthew 7:16–20 (emphasis added)

Roads have ditches on either side. On the road of Filled with God Himself, we have two ditches. On the one side, we have a ditch of stoic religious liturgy for the sake of tradition[8] that prohibits the move of the Spirit dangerously labelling it as demonic. In the other ditch, we have charismatic chaos where a believer's intimacy and maturity is based upon how intense or radical their manifestations of the Spirit appear.

Both are religious and both lack fruit.

Rather than having a faith that champions an appearance or form, let's champion faith that has an effect and bears fruit!

The Choice Is Yours

> *Where there are no oxen, the manger is clean, but abundant crops come by the strength of the ox.*
>
> —Proverbs 14:4

---

8 I'm not saying that liturgy is wrong. I'm saying that it's wrong if people worship it above the King it is supposed to point us to.

The author of this proverb gives a choice to the reader. He says that a clean stall is kept that way by not having an ox in it. He also says that a harvest comes from having an ox. He is asking a question: would you rather have a clean stall or a harvest?

That's the question the Lord put to me when I was coming out of my struggle with valuing the Holy Spirit in my ministry. Would you prefer a clean tidy church, or would you be willing to deal with the odd mess to reap a harvest? I have made my choice. What will yours be?

You can be filled with God Himself! You can walk in the abundance of heaven!

Pillar Prayer

Father, I thank You for Your Holy Spirit and I am asking that You give Him to me as my free gift of salvation. Holy Spirit, I want you to fill me and come into my heart. Baptize me in Your great power and fill me so that torrents of living water flow from me to the world around me. I pray that the world would be drenched with a flood from heaven. I repent for devaluing Your place in my life and heart and choose today for You to lead, guide, and empower me to be a witness for Jesus! I want to be filled with God Himself.

Thank You, Father, for Your lavish gift of the Holy Spirit. Thank You, Jesus, for purchasing my salvation with Your blood to make me a temple for the Holy Spirit. Thank you, Holy Spirit, for filling me and empowering me.

God, I am grateful for Your love. In Jesus' name, amen.

Pillar Confession

For I am not filled by Him, I am filled with Him (Acts 2:1–4, Ephesians 5:18). The Holy Spirit dwells within me (John 7:38–39, 1 Corinthians 3:16). My free gift from Jesus is the Holy Spirit (Acts 2:38), who enables me (1 Corinthians 12:4–11, Hebrews 2:4) to do every good work that He has planned for me this day (Ephesians 2:10).

chapter ten

Children with an Inheritance

In him we have obtained an inheritance, *having been predestined according to the purpose of him who works all things according to the counsel of his will, so that we who were the first to hope in Christ might be to the praise of his glory. In him you also, when you heard the word of truth, the gospel of your salvation, and believed in him,* were sealed with the promised Holy Spirit, who is the guarantee of our inheritance until we acquire possession of it, *to the praise of his glory.*

For this reason, because I have heard of your faith in the Lord Jesus and your love toward all the saints, I do not cease to give thanks for you, remembering you in my prayers, that the God of our Lord Jesus Christ, the Father of glory, may give you the Spirit of wisdom and of revelation in the knowledge of him, having the eyes of your hearts enlightened, that you may know what is the hope to which he has called you, what are the riches of his glorious inheritance in the saints, and what is the immeasurable greatness of his power toward us who believe, *according to the working of his great might...*
—Ephesians 1:11–19 (emphasis added)

OVER THE YEARS, I'VE BEGUN TO HAVE TROUBLE SEEING CLEARLY. I'M NOT losing my vision, but my focus seems to be a bit weaker. To correct this blurred vision, I have a pair of glasses. The lenses help me see clearly. Things that naturally are out of focus now have been corrected and are in proper focus.

I share this because the majority of believers need to have their reality shaped through the view of a new lens. In this chapter, I'd like to share a thought that will shape our worldview—a lens, if you will, that will help us move beyond the shortsightedness we so naturally slip into during the normality of life.

Two Conditions

This may seem like a bit of an oversimplification, but for the sake of understanding what the Lord has given to us I would like to look at the two major conditions of mankind.

We are all meant to be children of God. It is this beautiful Father's heart that all of mankind would be His children.

> *The Lord is not slow to fulfill his promise as some count slowness, but is patient toward you,* not wishing that any should perish, *but that all should reach repentance.*
>
> —2 Peter 3:9 (emphasis added)

At the same time, He is not interested in mindless robots created with no sense of personal awareness. So He gave mankind the incredible gift of free will. In His reckless love, He prefers to risk the pain of rejection so that He can have a relationship with children who have chosen Him versus those who mindlessly follow orders. God shows His desire for authentic love by giving us the freedom to choose Him of our own accord, letting His record and expression love stand on its own.

God shows His desire for authentic love by giving us the freedom to choose Him of our own accord, letting His record and expression love stand on its own.

Now, mankind has an adversary. This adversary is bent on misrepresenting the nature of God to trick us into questioning His character and thereby rejecting the expression of God's marvellous love. This adversary calls to account the fact that God's

131

mysterious ways can be difficult to see. Through half-truths and outright lies, he paints a picture of a distant, angry, vengeful judge who's looking for the opportunity to make our lives miserable and hopeless. He paints a picture of a God who finds man to be, at best, a creature to be tolerated, and at worst vermin to be obliterated.

In all of this, the enemy cries out, "Where is this loving God?"

God, in His infinite wisdom, made faith part of the equation of knowing Him—not to play hide-and-seek with us but to prepare man for the power of His expression of love.

> And without faith it is impossible to please him, *for whoever would draw near to God must believe that he exists and that he rewards those who seek him.*
>
> —Hebrews 11:6 (emphasis added)

His expression of love is the power of the cross, the culmination of the infinite love of God manifested in covenant toward mankind. To embrace the cross, the sacrifice of Jesus, is to become a part of an unbreakable covenant between the Father and mankind through our representative, Jesus.

The greatest mystery of the gospel is the power of the resurrection. To engage the covenant is to believe that Jesus rose from the dead, conquering sin and death. That is the only work that the Christian brings to the covenant. The Christian cannot earn salvation; it had to be provided. But the one work we must do to be saved is to believe.

> *Jesus answered them, "This is the work of God, that you believe in him whom he has sent."*
>
> —John 6:29

This covenant sets the stage for all mankind to enter into the very relationship Jesus has with the Father.

His Child

For you did not receive the spirit of slavery to fall back into fear, but you have received *the Spirit of adoption as sons, by whom we cry, "Abba! Father!" The Spirit himself bears witness with our spirit that we are children of God, and if children, then heirs—heirs of God and fellow heirs with Christ, provided we suffer with him in order that we may also be glorified with him.*

—Romans 8:15–17 (emphasis added)

The wonderful cross has provided man to be children in two major categories: either adopted children or orphans.

God places the solitary in families *and gives the desolate a home in which to dwell.*

—Psalm 68:6, AMPC (emphasis added)

Said another way, either you have a Father or you don't. Either you are saved or you are not.

In writing to the Romans, Paul uses this perspective to bring clarity to our relationship with God. The implications to the Romans would have been obvious. It would therefore be valuable to get some clarity of context for this thought about adoption.

In Rome, babies weren't sacred. It was important to a family for heirs to be acceptable. When a child was born, it was examined by the father. If it was undesirable in any way—the wrong sex, the wrong colour of eyes or hair, any deformities, weak in appearance— it could be left outside to die of exposure.

Satan's tactic of attacking the most vulnerable isn't limited to our present-day abortion crisis. Exposure was an acceptable form of discarding a baby. The undesirable child would be taken from its mother and left exposed at the garbage heap. The cries of dying babies were noted as background noise to citizens near the dump. These babies would eventually die, exposed to the elements, helpless, defenceless, and ultimately abandoned.

It was legal for a father to dispose of his child.

Roman law, however, had a unique perspective on adoption. If a wealthy citizen was without an heir, he could go amongst lower-caste families and find a suitable child. The young person would be chosen out of their humble condition and be given a new name. Their debts would be paid by their new father. They would be brought into their new father's home and written into the will to receive an inheritance.

By law, there had to be a witness of the adoption. The purpose of this was to ensure that the will could never be contested. When the adoptive father passed away, a witness of the adoption would come forward so that the extended family couldn't steal the inheritance. The witness would say, "I was a witness to the adoption of this child. It is legal and binding."

Another unique element of Roman adoption was that it was illegal to disown an adopted child. Unlike a natural child, who could be legally disposed of, an adoptive child could not be rejected.

These are the ramifications of the picture Paul painted for the Romans. You and I were orphans, without a father, without hope, and without an inheritance. We were left exposed and defenceless to the whims of the enemy. Mankind was left to receive its rightful judgement of death for being found flawed on account of sin. But God, through a covenant between the Father and Jesus, who represents mankind, witnessed by the Holy Spirit, made us benefactors of an incorruptible inheritance. God thus adopted mankind.

Please read the following scripture slowly. It's lengthy but worth meditating on. Read it from the perspective of Paul speaking of mankind.

Blessed be the God and Father of our Lord Jesus Christ, who has blessed us in Christ with every spiritual blessing in the heavenly places, even as he chose us in him before the foundation of the world, *that we should be holy and blameless before him.* In love he predestined us for adoption to himself as sons through Jesus Christ, *according to the purpose of his will, to the praise of his glorious grace, with which he has blessed us in the Beloved.* In him we have redemption through his blood, *the forgiveness of our trespasses, according to the riches of his grace, which he lavished upon us, in all wisdom and insight making known to us the mystery of his will, accord-ing to his purpose, which he set forth in Christ as a plan for the fullness of time, to unite all things in him, things in heaven and things on earth.*

In him we have obtained an inheritance, *having been pre-destined according to the purpose of him who works all things according to the counsel of his will, so that we who were the first to hope in Christ might be to the praise of his glory.* In him you also, when you heard the word of truth, the gospel of your salvation, and believed in him, were sealed with the promised Holy Spirit, who is the guarantee of our inheritance until we acquire possession of it, *to the praise of his glory.*

—Ephesians 1:3–14 (emphasis added)

We make the mistake of reading this verse from the perspective of the believer. However, Paul is speaking of mankind; he shifts gears to the believer in verse 11 and then makes clear in verse 13 that we took posses-sion of this gift by choosing salvation.

This is an important point.

God in the Lobby

I really enjoy the movie *Despicable Me*. Three little orphaned girls steal the heart of a dastardly criminal, who eventually adopts them and chang-es his ways. The story begins with the little girls living in the orphanage, hoping that someday they will be chosen by parents. One night, they pray before going to sleep for parents to come and choose them.

> There is a Father sitting in the lobby of the orphanage of mankind, waiting for any and every orphan to come out and be adopted. He has chosen us all and waits for the orphans to choose Him.

This is the cosmic mystery that Satan wants to keep hidden from the world. There is a Father sitting in the lobby of the orphanage of mankind, waiting for any and every orphan to come out and be adopted. He has chosen us all and waits for the orphans to choose Him.

Unbelievable. The orphans are no longer left to hope for a family. We get to choose the Father because He has already chosen us.

Remember when Jesus hung on the cross? He cried out something that has adoption ramifications:

> *And about the ninth hour Jesus cried out with a loud voice, saying, "Eli, Eli, lema sabachthani?" that is, "My God, my God, why have you forsaken me?*
>
> —Matthew 27:46

Because Jesus at that point was carrying the sin of mankind, many would say that the Father turned His face away from Jesus, and Jesus at that point felt the full extent of man's separation from God because of sin. I don't dispute that. I would like to add one perspective in light of our adoption because of the cross: God exposed Jesus.

This was all part of the necessary death of Jesus for this covenant to be fulfilled. But God, in legally exposing His Son, legally bound Himself through our adoption to never expose or disown us. And the enemy can never contest the will of God over our lives, because the Holy Spirit was there as the witness. Once we choose Him, we are His forever.

While I don't espouse a doctrine of eternal security in the sense of frivolous belief that has no apparent evidence of discipleship, I will say this: I think it's a lot harder to lose our salvation than the spirit of religion would like us to think.

Either we are sons of God or not. We are positioned either as adopted children or orphans. But sadly, many have embraced the cross but don't live in the promise, remaining in the mindset of orphans. In other words, they live as if they are natural children instead of children who have received a supernatural inheritance.

So let's look at our inheritance.

White Throne Judgement: Positional Inheritance

> *Then I saw a great white throne and him who was seated on it. From his presence earth and sky fled away, and no place was found for them.*

And I saw the dead, great and small, standing before the throne, and books were opened. Then another book was opened, which is the book of life. And the dead were judged by what was written in the books, according to what they had done. And the sea gave up the dead who were in it, Death and Hades gave up the dead who were in them, and they were judged, each one of them, according to what they had done. Then Death and Hades were thrown into the lake of fire. This is the second death, the lake of fire. And if anyone's name was not found written in the book of life, he was thrown into the lake of fire.

—Revelation 20:11–15

The White Throne Judgement will be the final destruction of sin, and the great separation of those who have chosen the cross and those who haven't. This judgement will be the end result of choosing to remain in the orphanage. It is both final and absolutely avoidable; the cross has saved mankind from the White Throne Judgement. God, through Jesus, gave us the freedom to choose life and our ultimate inheritance of heaven and eternal life. Through Jesus we are positioned to receive our inheritance. Even though we know this truth, it bears repeating.

For God so loved the world, that he gave his only Son, that whoever believes in him should not perish but have eternal life. For God did not send his Son into the world to condemn the world, but in order that the world might be saved through him.

—John 3:16–17

The Judgement Seat of Christ: Promised Inheritance

For we must all appear before the judgement seat of Christ, so that each one may receive what is due for what he has done in the body, whether good or evil.

—2 Corinthians 5:10

This judgement always frightened me. As I shared earlier, I told myself that one day I would stand before Jesus and the whole of heaven.

The video screen would light up and my life would be viewed for all of heaven's host to see. Every dark moment, every sin exposed. I would be shamed and embarrassed in front of the millions upon millions of saints, angels, and of course God Himself, judged harshly for my lack of holiness and for my sins.

This left me trying to impress the Lord with my works, trying to bank enough good works so that when this awful day came, perhaps I would have enough religious equity saved up that I could lessen my embarrassment and shame. Frankly, the teaching I had received hadn't disarmed my fears. If anything, what I was taught only affirmed that I was in for one serious cosmic spanking if I didn't save up some good works.

I was wrong. Let me remind you of the good news one more time: sin has been judged on the cross. You will not be judged for sin if you allowed the cross to be sin's judge on your behalf. This fear is one of the reasons so many live as orphans still; they think they are still evil. To bring clarity to that lie, I would respectfully return them to the "old man is dead" pillar.

However, as we will see in this pillar's connection to the elementary doctrines, God has prepared wonderful rewards for those who follow Jesus.

Renovated Thought: I Possess Access to All the Resources of Heaven

that the God of our Lord Jesus Christ, the Father of glory, may give you the Spirit of wisdom and of revelation in the knowledge of him, having the eyes of your hearts enlightened, that you may know what is the hope to which he has called you, what are the riches of his glorious inheritance in the saints, and what is the immeasurable greatness of his power toward us who believe, *according to the working of his great might*
—Ephesians 1:17–19 (emphasis added)

It would be difficult to fully understand the power of this verse without revisiting a perspective on the Holy Spirit we discussed earlier.

In him you also, when you heard the word of truth, the gospel of your salvation, and believed in him, were sealed with the promised Holy Spirit, who is the guarantee of our inheritance *until we acquire possession of it, to the praise of his glory.*

—Ephesians 1:13–14 (emphasis added)

The word guarantee carries the same concept as a down-payment. The Holy Spirit is given to us as a down-payment of our inheritance. To obtain a mortgage, I need to provide a down-payment. If it was ten percent of the whole, I would need ten percent to access the entirety of the funds.

Let's say you came to my home as a guest. For the sake of simplicity, let's say that my home is two thousand square feet. Ten percent of two thousand is two hundred. What would you think of my mental state if I invited you inside and you saw a bright orange tape line marking off two hundred square feet of the home? Perhaps that would amount to the front entryway and hall.

Of course, my wife and I would welcome you at the door and take your coat. You might look and see that our dining set was crammed into the hallway along with a bed. Confused, you might ask why the bed wasn't in the bedroom and the dining set not in the dining room. I might seriously reply, "We only paid for ten percent of the home, so we're only allowed to live in ten percent of the space."

We know that the down-payment gives us access to the entirety of the home, not just a percentage of it.

Here is where it gets fun for us. The true power of the down-payment of the Holy Spirit will start to make more sense.

Math (Again)

Earlier, I shared the mathematical fact that any number divided by infinity is zero.

...that the God of our Lord Jesus Christ, the Father of glory, may give you the Spirit of wisdom and of revelation in the knowledge

of him, *having the eyes of your hearts enlightened, that you may know what is the hope to which he has called you, what are the riches of his glorious inheritance in the saints,* and what is the immeasurable greatness of his power toward us who believe, *according to the working of his great might…*

—Ephesians 1:17–19 (emphasis added)

Heaven is an infinite inheritance. There's no possible percentage of the infinite that can be given as a guarantee.

So God gives us Himself in the Holy Spirit. In other words, God had to give us the infinite to have access to the infinite. You are filled with God Himself and therefore you have access to the entirety of your inheritance now.

So immeasurably great are the riches of heaven, your inheritance, and the greatness of His power that's available to you that nothing could be an adequate down-payment but the Immeasurable One Himself: the Holy Spirit.

You possess access to all of the resources of heaven. That is your inheritance.

Nevertheless, I tell you the truth: it is to your advantage that I go away, *for if I do not go away, the Helper will not come to you. But if I go, I will send him to you.*

—John 16:7 (emphasis added)

You and I have been given full access to our inheritance as God's children by the gift of precious Holy Spirit.

Let me put it one more way so we can fully engage the impact of this wonderful truth. I often tell people that there are two categories of the will of God: the known and the unknown.

The unknown will of God are those things that point to the direction of our lives. Where will I live? Who will I marry? What will my job/career/calling be? These are the day-to-day directional questions we would have of God in desiring to walk in His favour.

The known will of God, however, is His Word. Everything we need to know about the character and nature of God—His ways, His desires for us, and His expectations of us—is found in His Word. We are not left abandoned as to the nature of our Heavenly Father. His Book reveals what we need to know about Him.

Heaven's Promissory Note

And Peter said to them, "Repent and be baptized every one of you in the name of Jesus Christ for the forgiveness of your sins, and you will receive the gift of the Holy Spirit."

—Acts 2:38 (emphasis added)

The Bible, however, doesn't only consist of who God is and what He would expect. It is filled with promises He has made.

A promissory note is "a signed document containing a written promise to pay a stated sum to a specified person or the bearer at a specified date or on demand."[9]

The Word is a promissory note filled with written promises to the believer. Upon our choosing to believe in Jesus as Lord, we receive the gift of the Holy Spirit, the immeasurable Spirit of God, granting to us the immeasurable promises of God!

Glorified Response: Engaging a Missional Lifestyle (Works)

For by grace you have been saved through faith. And this is not your own doing; it is the gift of God, not a result of works, so that no one

---

9 *Google*, search results. Date of access: November 3 (https://www.google.ca/search?-client=safari&rls=en&q=promissory+note&ie=UTF-8&oe=UTF-8&gfe_rd=cr&ei=w-45pV8btLpHj-QOD54OIDQ).

may boast. For we are his workmanship, created in Christ Jesus for good works, which God prepared beforehand, that we should walk in them.

—Ephesians 2:8–10 (emphasis added)

The spirit of religion is committed to get us to work from a wrong perspective. That perspective is that we must *do* works to be saved. Paul addresses this in Ephesians 2 by separating the work of salvation from works as a result of salvation.

The work of salvation is not our own doing. We come to Jesus through belief in what He has done—by faith, so none of us can claim greater favour with God on account of our works. At the same time, God expects us to join Him in His mission of expressing and establishing His kingdom here on earth through us.

Sin Pays Wages

For the wages of sin is death, but the free gift of God is eternal life in Christ Jesus our Lord.

—Romans 6:23

In our society, work results in wages. You work for the day and are paid your wages for that day. Your wage is the result of the effort you put in working. Jesus threw a wrench into this mindset in the parable of the workers and the harvest.

For the kingdom of heaven is like a master of a house who went out early in the morning to hire laborers for his vineyard. After agreeing with the laborers for a denarius a day, he sent them into his vineyard. And going out about the third hour he saw others standing idle in the marketplace, and to them he said, "You go into the vineyard too, and whatever is right I will give you."

So they went. Going out again about the sixth hour and the ninth hour, he did the same. And about the eleventh hour he went out and found others standing. And he said to them, "Why do you stand here idle all day?"

They said to him, "Because no one has hired us."

He said to them, "You go into the vineyard too."

And when evening came, the owner of the vineyard said to his foreman, "Call the laborers and pay them their wages, beginning with the last, up to the first." And when those hired about the eleventh hour came, each of them received a denarius. Now when those hired first came, they thought they would receive more, but each of them also received a denarius. And on receiving it they grumbled at the master of the house, saying, "These last worked only one hour, and you have made them equal to us who have borne the burden of the day and the scorching heat."

But he replied to one of them, "Friend, I am doing you no wrong. Did you not agree with me for a denarius? Take what belongs to you and go. I choose to give to this last worker as I give to you. Am I not allowed to do what I choose with what belongs to me? Or do you begrudge my generosity?" So the last will be first, and the first last.

—Matthew 20:1–16 (emphasis added)

In this parable, we learn the difference between a wage and an inheritance.

When we feel that we're doing things for the Lord from a mindset of being paid for it, or earning a wage, we fall into the trap of sin. Sin pays wages; sons receive an inheritance. Said another way, we sin when we think we are earning our righteousness instead of living righteously.

That brings us to an important revelation about this often quoted passage in the Lord's prayer:

Your kingdom come, your will be done, on earth as it is in heaven.

—Matthew 6:10

We have reduced this prayer to an event-based perspective, as if we're hoping that some supernatural event will happen to point to His presence and kingdom being established here on Earth. Such thinking makes it appear that we're trying to establish a new form of government so that everyone will have to submit to the lordship of Jesus.

There will be a day when every knee will bow and tongue will confess that Jesus is Lord, but that day will be partnered with His appearing. Until then, His kingdom is coming to the earth to cause a confrontation between light and darkness for the sake of the knowledge of His glory to be revealed to the world. One person at a time.

> *For the earth will be filled with the* knowledge *of the glory of the* Lord *as the waters cover the sea.*
> —Habakkuk 2:14 (emphasis added)

What does this have to do with works?

As we will learn with the next pillar, we are meant to show the world the supernatural nature of this kingdom and express it through ministry to the world. Through entertainment, the world is crying out for the glory of the Lord to be revealed, and He has prepared works for us for that glory to be revealed.

Let me reiterate another point from earlier: you are the kingdom of heaven come to earth. Your interaction with the world around you is a kingdom experience for the world. You are an encounter with God. Your life, your obedience, your willingness to engage the works God has prepared for you are meant as encounters with God for the world.

> Your interaction with the world around you is a kingdom experience for the world.

> *Heal the sick in it and say to them, "The kingdom of God has come near to you."*
> —Luke 10:9

You are meant to be that encounter with the kingdom. It is not meant to be some sort of event that people observe, but rather a flesh-and-blood encounter through an ambassador from that kingdom.

Children with an Inheritance

All this is from God, who through Christ reconciled us to himself and gave us the ministry of reconciliation; that is, in Christ God was reconciling the world to himself, not counting their trespasses against them, and entrusting to us the message of reconciliation. Therefore, we are ambassadors for Christ, God making his appeal through us. We implore you on behalf of Christ, be reconciled to God.

—2 Corinthians 5:18–20 (emphasis added)

If it were a matter of establishing a form of earthly government, the Lord could do that without any issue. But His fervent desire is for people to choose Him individually, so that He can establish His adoptive love in every person. It's about salvation. He wants people saved, and He has chosen you and me to be the method by which it happens.

Performance's Bad Rap

And whatever you do, in word or deed, do everything in the name of the Lord Jesus, giving thanks to God the Father through him… Whatever you do, work heartily, as for the Lord and not for men, knowing that from the Lord you will receive the inheritance as your reward. You are serving the Lord Christ…

—Colossians 3:17, 23–24

So, whether you eat or drink, or whatever you do, do all to the glory of God.

—1 Corinthians 10:31

There's a difference between performing to be accepted and performing as a form of worship. Excellence gives glory to God and reflects the nature of the kingdom you represent. The orphan will perform in hopes that by impressing others, they will be accepted. The son or daughter performs knowing that they bring joy to their Father by doing their best.

Inheritance and Reward

We have to come to clarity on the difference between our inheritance and our rewards. In the above parable, Jesus shows us how the inheritance of heaven is released. The workers in the parable said to the master of the house, *"These last worked only one hour, and you have made them equal to us who have borne the burden of the day and the scorching heat"* (Matthew 20:12). The master then replied,

> *"Friend, I am doing you no wrong. Did you not agree with me for a denarius? Take what belongs to you and go. I choose to give to this last worker as I give to you. Am I not allowed to do what I choose with what belongs to me? Or do you begrudge my generosity?" So the last will be first, and the first last.*
>
> —Matthew 20:13–16

One's timeline in accepting the lordship of Jesus has no determination on their share of the inheritance. Whether faith is lived out for one's whole life or found on one's death bed, both will have an equal share in the wonder of their heavenly inheritance.

Rewards, however, are given to those who have run their race.

> *For I am already being poured out as a drink offering, and the time of my departure has come. I have fought the good fight, I have finished the race, I have kept the faith. Henceforth there is laid up for me the crown of righteousness, which the Lord, the righteous judge, will award to me on that day, and not only to me but also to all who have loved his appearing.*
>
> —2 Timothy 4:6–8

In the parable of the talents, Jesus helps us to understand the way God rewards His children. A master gives his slaves some talents to do business with until he returns. Upon his return, he asks for an accounting of the talents he gave his slaves.

Children with an Inheritance

Now after a long time the master of those servants came and settled accounts with them. And he who had received the five talents came forward, bringing five talents more, saying, "Master, you delivered to me five talents; here, I have made five talents more." His master said to him, "Well done, good and faithful servant. You have been faithful over a little; I will set you over much. Enter into the joy of your master." And he also who had the two talents came forward, saying, "Master, you delivered to me two talents; here, I have made two talents more." His master said to him, "Well done, good and faithful servant. You have been faithful over a little; I will set you over much. Enter into the joy of your master."

—Matthew 25:19–23

"Enter into the joy of your master." It is the Father's unbridled joy to reward His children! One is an inheritance given out of immeasurable love; the other is a reward given out of unbridled joy.

Our inheritance (heaven) is what the Father wants to give all mankind. For that reason, it remains an equal share for all who come to a saving knowledge of Jesus. However, rewards are the joyful response of the Father for a life worthy of the Father's "Well done."

The Connection: Eternal Judgement

This pillar is connected to the elementary doctrine of eternal judgement.

For we must all appear before the judgement seat of Christ, so that each one may receive what is due for what he has done in the body, whether good or evil.

—2 Corinthians 5:10

As we have already discussed, our eternal judgement (the Judgement Seat of Christ, or the Bema Seat) is a judgement of reward. The word "evil" used in the passage above is better rendered "worthless". Works will be judged on the merit of both intention and one's obedience to act.

He Already Said Yes

On that day many will say to me, "Lord, Lord, did we not prophesy in your name, and cast out demons in your name, and do many mighty works in your name?" And then will I declare to them, "I never knew you; depart from me, you workers of lawlessness."
—Matthew 7:22–23

So how do we know what to do? How do we discern what works are authorized and unauthorized? What is worthless and what is worthwhile? Jesus gave us a hint as to what sort of works we should do:

I will give you the keys of the kingdom of heaven; and whatever you bind (declare to be improper and unlawful) on earth must be what is already bound *in heaven; and whatever you loose (declare lawful) on earth must be what* is already loosed *in heaven.*
—Matthew 16:19, AMPC (emphasis added)

Often we try to discern what Jesus is saying without trying to find out what He has already said. We need to look for what Jesus has already said yes to, and do those things.

God Wants to Reward You

We sometimes think God is stingy, or that He prefers to withhold from us. Nothing could be further from the truth. It's just that His rewards are primarily eternal. While He does reward obedience on earth, His reward is located where moth and rust cannot corrupt (Luke 12:33).

Think of it this way. In the stock market, there are two forms of return on your investment. There is stock that you purchase at a low price; over time, the investment grows on account of its increasing value on the market. There is also stock that you purchase at a set price; as its market value increases, you receive dividends. One increases in value, the other pays out on the increase of its value.

In the same way, there are times when our obedience goes directly to our "account" in heaven, and heaven will determine the value and return. In other situations, heaven deems that a dividend on that obedience will bring you the best return on your investment and be the most beneficial to you.

Here's a quick reminder as to the out-of-balance return God has in store for you:

> ...*having the eyes of your hearts enlightened, that you may know what is the hope to which he has called you, what are the* riches of his glorious inheritance *in the saints, and what is the* immeasurable greatness *of his power toward us who believe, according to the working of his great might*...
> —Ephesians 1:18–19 (emphasis added)

> *But, as it is written, "What no eye has seen, nor ear heard,* nor the heart of man imagined, what God has prepared for those who love him"...
> —1 Corinthians 2:9 (emphasis added)

God gives us a hint of His extravagant nature in the expression of His love for us as children. It leads me to wonder: if He loves so freely, how much more freely will He reward?

Crowns in Heaven

> ...*the twenty-four elders fall down before him who is seated on the throne and worship him who lives forever and ever. They cast their crowns before the throne, saying*...
> —Revelation 4:10

The Bible clearly shows us what one form of reward will be in heaven: crowns. There are five crowns of reward given to those who have followed Christ.

The Crown of Righteousness. This crown is the reward for those who have lived lives that are truly acts of worship towards the Lord. Righteous and holy living will not go without their reward.

> *Henceforth there is laid up for me* the crown of righteousness, *which the Lord, the righteous judge, will award to me on that day, and not only to me but also to all who have loved his appearing.*
> —2 Timothy 4:8 (emphasis added)

Note the difference between being made righteous and acts of righteousness. Heaven is the reward for being made righteous through our belief in the work of the cross. This crown, however, is a reward for acts of righteousness. Not religious works in hope of acceptance, but rather righteous acts we do because of our acceptance as sons and daughters. These are activities, behaviours, and lifestyles that reflect the nature of heaven.

> *...who by faith conquered kingdoms,* performed acts of righteousness, *obtained promises, shut the mouths of lions...*
> —Hebrews 11:33, NASB (emphasis added)

This refers to those sweet people who have lived their lives with heaven in mind.

The Crown of Rejoicing. This is known also as the Soul Winner's Crown, the crown given to those whose passionate love for the lost and purposed lifestyle bring people to a saving knowledge of Jesus.

> *For what is our hope or joy or* crown of boasting *before our Lord Jesus at his coming? Is it not you? For you are our glory and joy.*
> —1 Thessalonians 2:19–20 (emphasis added)

To the evangelist who for years has felt misunderstood, God will vindicate you for your love for the lost with a crown that matches the beauty of heaven's rejoicing.

Just so, I tell you, there is joy before the angels of God over one sinner who repents.

—Luke 15:10

The Incorruptible Crown. This is the crown rewarded to those who have overcome obstacles, whether through exercising self-control over sin and sinful habits or facing adversity for the sake of the call of God.

Do you not know that in a race all the runners run, but only one receives the prize? So run that you may obtain it. Every athlete exercises self-control in all things. They do it to receive a perishable wreath, but we an imperishable. *So I do not run aimlessly; I do not box as one beating the air. But I discipline my body and keep it under control, lest after preaching to others I myself should be disqualified.*

—1 Corinthians 9:24–27 (emphasis added)

This is a reward for heavenward focus through adversity or temptation. Perhaps you have felt forgotten in the sacrifices you've made out of obedience to the kingdom. Or perhaps you have felt the sting of condemnation for continually facing the same temptation over and over and fighting hard to conquer it.

There is a crown for you.

The Crown of Life. This is known as the Martyr's Crown.

Blessed is the man who remains steadfast under trial, for when he has stood the test he will receive the crown of life, *which God has promised to those who love him.*

—James 1:12 (emphasis added)

It will be the reward for those who have persevered through trial and tribulation. It will be for those who have been faithful even unto death. It is the eternal reward for pain and suffering. It will be the reward for those who showed no greater love than to lay down their lives for another.

The Crown of Glory. This is also known as the Shepherd's Crown. It will be the reward for those who lead the people of God through the fivefold offices.

> *So I exhort the elders among you, as a fellow elder and a witness of the sufferings of Christ, as well as a partaker in the glory that is going to be revealed: shepherd the flock of God that is among you, exercising oversight, not under compulsion, but willingly, as God would have you; not for shameful gain, but eagerly; not domineering over those in your charge, but being examples to the flock. And when the chief Shepherd appears, you will receive the unfading crown of glory.*
> —1 Peter 5:1–4 (emphasis added)

Perhaps, Pastor, you have felt like your role isn't honoured by those you lead. Or perhaps you feel that the hours you spend in preparation to preach and teach the Word have fallen on deaf ears. Heaven has seen, heard, and will reward those who have faithfully loved, led, and taught His flock in the ways of the kingdom.

I find myself struck by the wonder of God's love and grace when I look at these crowns that await people who have lived their lives with heaven in mind.

Renewed Focus

I started this chapter by sharing about how my eyes need help focusing, that I need a lens to help me see things clearly. Many Christians have lost sight of the fact that God is prepared to reward them for their obedience. I find it fascinating that He has prepared an inheritance for me, and that I get to participate in its growth through simple obedience.

Perhaps you have grown weary and have forgotten about the eternal ramifications of your obedience. Perhaps it is time to return to viewing your life through the lens of eternity.

You are a child with an inheritance.

Pillar Prayer

Father, I thank You that I am adopted. I thank You that You love me extravagantly and that You reward me in the same way. I thank You that I am securely established as Your child and securely established as Your heir. I ask that You renew my mind and establish my understanding in this: I am Your child and You will reward me.

I repent for being short-sighted in my living and in my obedience to You. I choose to say yes to what You are saying yes to, and to live today with eternity in mind.

I thank You that You are rewarding me and that You are going to reward me for my obedience. I pray that I would have an encounter with the kingdom of heaven today.

I thank you that you are a rewarder of those who seek You, and I choose to seek You today. In Jesus' wonderful name, amen.

Pillar Confession

I am loved by God and I am His child (1 John 3:1). I am purchased by His blood (Ephesians 1:7) and my inheritance is heaven (Ephesians 1:11). Through the gift of the Holy Spirit (Acts 2:38), I have access today to all of the resources of heaven (Ephesians 1:13–14). I am not an orphan (John 14:18); I am adopted and an heir (Romans 8:15–17). Through Jesus I am positioned to receive all blessings—spiritually (Ephesians 1:3), emotionally (Philippians 4:7, Ephesians 3:16–17), and physically (Matthew 6:25–34, Philippians 4:19)—from my Father who is in heaven (Matthew 6:9).

chapter eleven

Naturally Supernatural

You are the salt of the earth, but if salt has lost its taste, how shall its saltiness be restored? It is no longer good for anything except to be thrown out and trampled under people's feet.

You are the light of the world. *A city set on a hill cannot be hidden. Nor do people light a lamp and put it under a basket, but on a stand, and it gives light to all in the house. In the same way,* let your light shine before others, so that they may see your good works and give glory to your Father who is in heaven.

—Matthew 5:13–16 (emphasis added)

It was going to be one of *those* Sundays.

It was a cold February morning. We were trying to get a new sound board to function properly and the worship team was frustrated with the way the sound check and rehearsal had gone. My microphone was squeaking and there was feedback every time I spoke. It seemed that anything that could go wrong did go wrong.

The pre-service prayer was full of stress and anxiety. The whole time I felt like it would be a miracle if we survived the service, let alone have God move amongst us.

Yes, one of *those* Sundays.

Then I met her.

One of our Filipino members brought me to the foyer to meet one of the friends she had invited to come to church that day. The friend's name was Sally, a young mother in her twenties with a son. Like many of the Filipino people in my church, she was in Canada working to make money for family back in in the Philippines. However, while she was here she had gotten ill.

It had started with a pain in the back of her knees, and slowly the pain became numbness and moved down to her feet. After some time, and visiting baffled doctors, the numbness continued up her legs all the way to her chest, leaving her paralyzed in a wheelchair. The doctors couldn't explain what was wrong and her physiotherapists had told her that therapy was no longer going to be any benefit due to her paralysis. Her legs had begun to atrophy and there was no guarantee that the paralysis wasn't going to continue to move up her body.

That's how I met her.

I shook her hand, welcomed her, and walked back into the sanctuary. Already frustrated because of the other issues we were facing, I complained to God about how I hated when people came to my church in wheelchairs, because they left in their wheelchairs.

As the service went on, I felt that we needed to pray for people who were in need of healing. I invited folks to respond to the call and come to the altar where our elders and ministry team could pray for them.

Sally wheeled herself to the front and stopped at the right side of the altar.

Being the man of faith that I am, I went over to the left side to pray for headaches and tummy aches. I was like Jonah, running away. The Lord spoke, telling me to go back to the other side of the altar and join the others who were praying for Sally. As I reluctantly obeyed, He reminded me of a YouTube video I had recently seen from Mobile, Alabama where a pastor's wife, who had been paralyzed for many years, had been healed and walked again. I had watched that video with tears streaming down my face, longing for it to happen in my life.

What happened next changed me forever. But more on that a little later.

Sing for Me

I heard a joke recently about a young man who fell in love with the voice of an opera singer as he listened to her recordings. Although they had never met, he fell in love with her because of the rapturous tones of her singing. Her voice expressed such vibrant, youthful beauty.

While listening to one of her recordings, he could bear it no longer. His love for her burned white-hot and he managed to contact her through email to express his undying love and his great desire to marry her. She responded that she was recently widowed and quite lonely. Indeed, she was at an age in her life when it would be foolish to wait longer.

So she accepted his proposal and they set a wedding date.

When his new bride walked down the aisle, he could see that she was somewhat older than her voice had let on, but his love for her grew as she sang to him while coming toward the altar. They were married.

As she prepared for their wedding night, he noticed that she was taking off a wig to reveal thinning silver hair. She took out her wooden eye, placed her false teeth in a cup of water, and unhooked a wooden leg. Leaning the leg against the door, she donned a flannel nightgown and began to hop toward the bed.

Seeing his new bride hopping toward the bed, the young man cried out, "Sing for me! Please! Sing for me!"

Not Like Moses

Paul wrote to the Corinthians about the glory of the ministry of the Spirit. In 2 Corinthians 3, he compares the glory with the way Moses' face shone when he was given the first covenant, carved in stone. In talking of the permanence of the glory of the Spirit, he says,

> *Since we have such a hope, we are very bold,* not like Moses, who would put a veil over his face *so that the Israelites might not gaze at the outcome of what was being brought to an end.*
> —2 Corinthians 3:12–13 (emphasis added)

Recently, Cathy noticed something about Moses that I hadn't seen before:

> *When* Moses came down from Mount Sinai, *with the two tablets of the testimony in his hand as he came down from the mountain,* Moses did not know that the skin of his face shone because he had been talking with God. *Aaron and all the people of Israel saw* Moses, and behold, the skin of his face shone, and they were afraid to come near him. *But Moses called to them, and Aaron and all the leaders of the congregation returned to him, and Moses talked with them. Afterward all the people of Israel came near, and he commanded them all that the Lord had spoken with him in Mount Sinai.* And when Moses had finished speaking with them, he put a veil over his face.
>
> Whenever Moses went in before the Lord to speak with him, he would remove the veil, until he came out. *And when he came out and told the people of Israel what he was commanded,* the people of Israel would see the face of Moses, that the skin of Moses' face was shining. And Moses would put the veil over his face again, until he went in to speak with him.
>
> —Exodus 34:29–35 (emphasis added)

Although it's well known, it still amazes me that Moses' face shone when he came down from speaking with the Lord. The part I hadn't seen before is that his face didn't stop shining. Afterward, whenever he went into the tent of meeting to talk with the Lord, he would take the veil off, but when he'd come out to see the people he would cover his face again.

So, why would Paul tell us not to be like Moses? As Jesus said, we are the light of the world, and we are supposed to shine our light before men, so they will see our good works and glorify our Father in heaven (Matthew 5:16).

How do we shine? Through works that glorify God. Jesus showed us how.

And Jesus went throughout all the cities and villages, teaching in their synagogues and proclaiming the gospel of the kingdom and healing every disease and every affliction.

—Matthew 9:35

It's natural for us to be supernatural. It has become the normal activity of the church to preach but not to demonstrate. Jesus went about preaching and teaching and then demonstrating the nature of the kingdom He was representing. The natural order of heaven is to eradicate every form of dysfunction, whether it be physical, emotional, or spiritual.

We have more than a message; we have the miraculous. Look at what it says in 2 Peter:

> It has become the normal activity of the church to preach but not to demonstrate.

His divine power has granted to us all things that pertain to life and godliness, *through the knowledge of* him who called us to his own glory and excellence, *by which he has granted to us his precious and very great promises,* so that through them you may become partakers of the divine nature, *having escaped from the corruption that is in the world because of sinful desire.*

—2 Peter 1:3–4 (emphasis added)

It stands to reason that if we are able to be filled with God Himself through the baptism of the Holy Spirit, we can also be enabled to operate in the supernatural ways of God. In 2 Peter 1:3–4, He calls us into His own glory and excellence and grants us promises that enable us to partake in His divine nature. That means we become like Him.

Moses' skin didn't shine because of its reflective properties. Our skin is not a mirror. We are not like the moon, shining because we are shined on. I once heard Bill Johnson say that, like light bulbs, we are made to shine. We just need to be connected to the power. The most natural thing that a light bulb does is shine.

Arise, shine, for your light has come, and the glory of the Lord has risen upon you. For behold, darkness shall cover the earth, and thick darkness the peoples; but the Lord will arise upon you, and his glory will be seen upon you. And nations shall come to your light, and kings to the brightness of your rising.

—Isaiah 60:1–3

There is great darkness in the world, but the glory of the Lord is meant to be seen on us. The nations will see light, *your* light, and come to it. Your light. Jesus told us to let our light shine. This light brings hope, freedom, health, and provision, and it connects mankind with his Creator and the Provider of all. That is your light. It is Christ in you, the hope of glory. It is the joyful anticipation of what is known to be good.

The song of religion is no longer enough for the world. The song may be beautiful, but up close, it is aged and flawed. The world is not like the young man. The nations will not come to the sound of a pretty song; they want the light! They want to see the glory of the Lord, not just hear about it. Like the young man who asked his new bride to sing, the world is crying out for us to shine.

It's a Fear Thing

The children of Israel feared what they saw on Moses' face. Because they were afraid, Moses hid the glory of God that shone from his skin. The fear was there for good reason. God's holiness, His righteousness, was unattainable for man. They knew that His glory was deadly to those whose nature was to sin. They were justifiably afraid.

Theirs was a covenant of law. Ours is of grace.

That's why Paul wrote in 2 Corinthians 3 about the wonderful glory of the second covenant. The grace of God was manifested through the work of Jesus on the cross, and then mercy triumphed over justice. Mankind has no need to fear God's glory any longer. The atonement has been accomplished through Jesus and *it is finished!*

Therefore, the light that once caused mankind to tremble in fear can now become a beacon of hope for the nations to come into wholeness.

159

And you are that light.

Jesus said to not put your light under a bucket. You were meant to be seen. You were meant to light up the world around you. You have within you the power of God to bring freedom to your circle of influence.

We have to come into agreement with heaven on this principle if we're going to walk in the openness of heaven. You are naturally supernatural. There is no longer a difference between your natural side and your supernatural side. You are partaking in the divine nature that Peter wrote about.

What a way to think! What a way to live! Know that you are not only entirely forgiven, but entirely equipped to be an agent of freedom over every work of wickedness the enemy could devise.

Time to Pray for Judgement

Jesus described an interesting responsibility of the Holy Spirit:

> *And when he comes, he will convict the world concerning sin and righteousness and judgement: concerning sin, because they do not believe in me; concerning righteousness, because I go to the Father, and you will see me no longer; concerning judgement, because the ruler of this world is judged.*

—John 16:8–11

This is so great. The Holy Spirit is here on earth to bring about some convictions. Firstly, a conviction for the sinner so they can come to the place of freedom in Jesus. Secondly, a conviction of righteousness to help the disciple discern the rightness of his actions. And finally, a conviction of the judgement of God... on the devil.

One Sunday morning, I asked our prophetic leader, Kayle Mumby, to open our service. He brought this truth to reality when he opened the service in a jarring fashion. He said, "I invite the judgement of the Lord in this house this morning." I was stunned and began to think of ways to help fix the mess that my friend had made. Then he said this: "I invite the judgement of God on cancer, MS, sickness, pain, and suffering." He continued to name many other works of the enemy against mankind, and I began to weep with joy.

Yes, Lord! Bring your judgement on cancer, sickness, depression, and mental illness! Bring your judgement on poverty, injustice, slavery, and abuse. Bring the full measure of your judgement on the enemy!

He wants to do that very thing. And He wants to do it through you.

The Connection

This pillar is connected to the elementary doctrinal principle of the laying on of hands. The deceiver, the counterfeiter, again observes a principle of heaven and perverts it.

Touch Me; I'm Contagious!

Sickness and disease can be contagious. Touch someone with a contagious sickness and you may get sick as well. There is a transfer that happens through touch. So, too, can the transfer of the power of God come through touch. While miracles happened in several other ways through Jesus, for saints today it starts in the realm of touch.

The touch of the disciple connects lost mankind to the love of God and releases God's judgement on the work of the enemy against lost mankind.

We need to touch our world. We need to touch those around us with the supernatural nature of the kingdom that holds our citizenship.

So then you are no longer strangers and aliens, but you are fellow citizens with the saints and members of the household of God…
—Ephesians 2:19

When a citizen is in a foreign land, his embassy is a safe haven and he can avail himself of all the rights and privileges of his home country. I am Canadian. If I were in another country but wanted to avail myself of the privileges of my Canadian citizenship, I would go to the Canadian embassy and my government would operate on my behalf.

We are citizens of heaven, but we don't need an embassy to access the privileges of our citizenship. All we need is to open heaven over the earth.

The earth is the Lord's and the fullness thereof, the world and those who dwell therein...

—Psalms 24:1

Renovated Thought: I Can Do All Things through Christ

I can do all things through him who strengthens me.

—Philippians 4:13

The supernatural power of God at work in you is also meant to work through you. The key is believing that it can.

Through Christ, we are enabled to do all things.

It is a tragedy that people can be Christians their whole lives and not witness or experience the power of God. Like the young man and the opera singer, they have only known the sound of the song (the stories) but have never experienced the wonder of God and the immeasurable greatness of His power towards those who believe (Ephesians 2:19).

You are naturally supernatural. Anything less is a misrepresentation of God's kingdom. Through Jesus, you have access to the power of God for the world around you.

> You are naturally supernatural. Anything less is a misrepresentation of God's kingdom.

Chaining Elephants

Elephants are huge. I took my kids to a circus once and they got to ride an elephant. It was so cool to see them way up there on its back. In places like India, where elephants are used for work, the people have devised an interesting way to keep elephants from running off. The elephants wear a collar around one of their legs and are chained to a stake or tree.

A massive, powerful animal held by a tiny chain? How can this be?

When an elephant is a calf, its handler will chain it like I described above. It will struggle against the chain to get free, but because it's a calf it isn't strong enough to break the chain or the tree. After some time and many attempts to free itself, there comes a point when the elephant tires and believes that it will never break free.

When the elephant matures into an adult, even though their great strength is obvious, as far as the elephant is concerned, it can never break that chain. So it never tries.

Do not reduce your capacity to what you think you're capable of. We so often allow ourselves to be duped into thinking our capacity is restricted by our ability. Even with my very best concentration, I cannot will someone to get even one percent better. I cannot with my own power change the circumstances of any person one iota. It's all God, but He wants to do it all through me.

He brings the all; you bring the you. Since His all is in you, you are naturally supernatural. Let Him put His super on your natural and watch what happens.

Partners

> Working together with him, *then, we appeal to you not to receive the grace of God in vain.*
> —2 Corinthians 6:1 (emphasis added)

In Chapter Nine, we discussed cohabitating with the Holy Spirit. I'd like to share how this pillar, being naturally supernatural, describes how we co-labour with Him.

What does it mean to co-labour? It means that we are working together.

> *So then the Lord Jesus, after he had spoken to them, was taken up into heaven and sat down at the right hand of God.* And they went out and preached everywhere, while the Lord worked with them and confirmed the message by accompanying signs.
> —Mark 16:19–20 (emphasis added)

The co-labouring between us and our Father is a partnership. When I want to wash my car, I take a garden hose and attach it to the outdoor tap on my house. That tap is in my backyard and only sticks out a couple of inches from the foundation of the house, making it impossible for me to drive my car underneath it. So I use a garden hose.

The hose isn't the source of water; it is a conduit for water. In the same way, I am not the source of power. That perspective alone protects me from pride getting in the way, and at the same time allows me to operate from rest, knowing that I cannot manufacture the miraculous, though I am necessary in its delivery. Because of my willingness to co-labour with the Lord, His power flows through me to the world around me.

When we co-labour with God, He puts His super on our natural, extending His kingdom to those we touch.

> *...while God also bore witness by signs and wonders and various miracles and by gifts of the Holy Spirit distributed according to his will.*
> —Hebrews 2:4

Glorified Response: Embracing a Life of Miracles (Risk)

> *And when they had prayed, the place in which they were gathered together was shaken, and they were all filled with the Holy Spirit and continued to speak the word of God with boldness.*
> —Acts 4:31

One of the overlooked evidences of the Holy Spirit's baptism is boldness. The believers of the early church operated in signs and wonders and were able to share the gospel with their world because they were bold. That boldness led to them being willing to take risks.

The expression of the supernatural nature of the kingdom of God will not happen if we aren't willing to take risks. James wrote that faith without works is dead. I would like to suggest to you that faith without risk is impossible. Risk is the primary ingredient in a recipe for faith. The difference between the Christian who takes faith risks and the Christian who doesn't is that one will have *experience* in the miracles of the Lord, while the other will have *knowledge* of the miracles of the Lord.

Which are you?

To hear this message and not respond to it is to be blinded by forgetfulness.

> But be doers of the word, and not hearers only, *deceiving yourselves. For if anyone is a hearer of the word and not a doer, he is like a man who looks intently at his natural face in a mirror.* For he looks at himself and goes away and at once forgets what he was like.
> —James 1:22–24 (emphasis added)

So many believers go to their church on a Sunday morning and have an amazing time of worship, raising their voices and their hands. They shout praise and proclaim "Amen" to their pastor's message. They leave invigorated, excited, filled up, and challenged to take the world for Jesus.

Once lunch starts to digest, they enjoy their Sunday snooze. The image of the way they are supposed to live fades, and they forget what they really look like and live out a dim reflection of the kingdom they belong to, living under the oppressive cloud of demonic activity over them, not being transformed by heaven but by the natural.

Superman would dress like the mild-mannered reporter Clark Kent to hide his real identity. Beneath the awkward veneer of a clumsy, soft-spoken reporter was the mighty man of steel. It would seem pretty ridiculous for Superman to forget that he was Superman when he dressed like Clark. Suddenly, in the midst of an attack from Lex Luthor, imagine Clark looking to the sky with the rest of the citizens of Metropolis and hoping for Superman to streak in and save the day.

So many Christians cover their true identity by being mild-mannered, religious, nice people, hiding who they really are for fear of what the world might think. Don't forget what you look like. You look like heaven. You are shining. Don't hide it any longer. Take a risk. Be bold.

The world doesn't need Clark Kent.

Hollywood Is Crying Out

We need to pay more attention to the prophetic cry of entertainment. You can often see the confusion of the world through media.

At the time of this writing, there are so many movies about the supernatural. Vampires, zombies, werewolves, and superheroes. Why? We tend to look at it through our religious lens and declare how demonic it is or how it's rooted in foolish fantasy. We end up missing the cry of our world.

Why vampires? Because they know that there's something about the blood, but they can't put their finger on it. Why zombies? Because they know they're the walking dead but don't know for sure what that means or how to come to full life. They know that there's something about being dead and coming to life but can't make sense of it all. Why werewolves? They know that there is something about transformation, but they're unclear about how it works. Why superheroes? They know they are supposed to have an otherworldly power. They know that the power is meant to be here amongst us but they don't know how it's supposed to manifest.

And here we are, those who know the power of the blood, the wonder of resurrection life, the great transformation to newness of life and mind and the great power of the anointing of the Holy Spirit, revealing a supernatural power that is available to all.

What are we doing with it?

Take the Risk

What if nothing happens?

A friend of mine, Craig Buroker, spoke at my church a while back and said, "If nothing happens, then they are the same as when you met them. But if something does happen…"

The fear of failure will prevent you from risking being bold. Jesus healed all. I am nowhere near that happening in my life and ministry. But Wayne Gretzky once said that you are sure to never score on a hundred percent of the shots you don't take. The same goes for the believer. You are sure to see no breakthrough in a hundred percent of the risks you don't take.

Being willing to face failure is the most important part. I've heard it said that if you fail to plan, you plan to fail. I agree with that, but I've decided in my life that I need to plan to fail a bit more often. If I don't put myself in positions that will lead to failure without God moving on my behalf, I am not willing to take risks. Now, I'm not talking about being foolhardy and falling into the temptation Satan tried to catch Jesus in when he asked Jesus to jump off the temple. I'm saying that if I make sure all my plans can be accomplished in my strength, I've taken risk out of the equation, negating myself from operating in faith.

I'll build on this statement in the next chapter, but we have to understand that unanswered prayers prepare our character to steward the answered ones.

Why? Not seeing what we're believing for will lead us to two different behaviours. On the one hand, people disengage from risk and shrink back to a place of belief in God from a perspective of what He isn't doing. Others will press into intimacy with Him, not satisfied with their unanswered prayer as a representation of God's goodness. That intimacy will build character and turn a miracle into an opportunity to worship rather than an opportunity to promote ourselves.

If we're not prepared in our character, the power of God moving through us can be destructive by leading us into self-reliance and pride. But when God intervenes and miraculously moves on your behalf, the season of unanswered prayers will have prepared you to be able to manage the answered ones. Why? Because a miracle will cause you to worship rather than want to be worshiped.

What Risks Do I Take?

Intimacy will protect you from taking unauthorized risks. Doing things for God without having intimacy with God is unadvised (see Matthew 7:21–23). The closer we are in relationship with Him, the better we will hear His voice and know His heart. The greater our level of intimacy, the more we can be trusted to reflect His heart.

In the early stages of our discipleship, we need to walk from the perspective of seeking permission. However, as we grow we become safe to trust with His power.

Miracles aren't for us. They are for those who need the miracles. We often internalize the miraculous for our benefit, forgetting that it's the person we're praying for who needs the miracle. We will feel stronger in our faith if we see what we're asking for, forgetting that the person asking for it has the greater need. That's the difference between being moved by compassion and being moved by compulsion.

Our compassion will lead us to not stop until we receive an answer; compulsion will internalize the issue and lead us to be self-serving. It will be about our faith, our prayer, and the need of the individual we're praying for will become secondary.

Take risks that will bring glory to Jesus. Avoid risks that bring glory to you.

Where Do I Begin?

You might be feeling a bit overwhelmed by all of this "attack the impossible" talk. Maybe for you, praying out loud would be a supernatural event. How do we start this process of being naturally supernatural?

Paul wrote to the church to give us a hint as to how to engage a supernatural lifestyle.

> *Pursue love, and earnestly desire the spiritual gifts, especially that you may prophesy.*
>
> —1 Corinthians 14:1

Prophesy is the entry level into the supernatural. It is still very much a risk to share an impression from God with someone, but the confirmation of their response will bolster your confidence in hearing and obeying His voice.

There is no different in His eyes between sharing an encouraging word ("I feel God saying that He wants you to know that He loves you") and commanding someone in a wheelchair to stand and walk. For us, however, there seems like a monumental difference! And that is the point of entering through the gate of prophecy into a lifestyle of the supernatural.

As we learn to hear the voice of God for what He is saying to others, and learning how do deliver what He says, we develop confidence to continue obeying Him at what would appear to be greater assignments.

I realize it's hard for us to comprehend this, but to the Lord there is no differing measures of the miraculous, because He is supernatural. Everything He does in miraculous. That is His normal, so He doesn't look at one supernatural event as requiring more power than another. His infinite nature never requires a counting of the cost. To the infinite, there is no such thing as a price tag. Neither is there any waste. God's power is never taxed or depleted. He never needs to regroup after a miracle or rest a bit to get ready for the next one.

He is power, so your act of obedience in the prophetic is in the same arena as the miraculous. They are both supernatural events.

Much has been written about prophesying, but let me give you a few hints to get you started on a healthy path.

Nature of Prophecy

There is the gift of prophecy and the office of the prophet, according to Ephesians 4:11–12. Unfortunately, due to insecurity, people are constantly trapped into pursuing a platform and identity rather than simply walking in the gift.

Someone will begin to walk in the gift of prophecy, but then they'll begin to wonder if they are in the office of the prophet, so they'll start to use their gift as a way to create a platform for themselves. The office gifts require the anointing, but also the appointing. You need to obviously be anointed in the prophetic to qualify for the office, but at the same time a seasoned appointed leader will have to appoint you to that office. None who operate in the office gifts are self-made people.

How to Prophesy

On the other hand, the one who prophesies speaks to people for their
upbuilding and encouragement and consolation.
—1 Corinthians 14:3

Prophecy has three main components. Upbuilding (edification), encouragement, and consolation (comfort). When we deliver a prophetic word, it needs to fit into one of these categories. Many people make the mistake of assuming that the prophetic is meant for correction. The problem with this perspective is that correction presumes authority over an individual. This is how people can get off-track and move into controlling or manipulating others. Scores of people have been wounded by such expressions of the prophetic.

The whole purpose of being prophetic is to lovingly serve others through edifying, encouraging, and comforting them. The prophetic is meant to reflect the nature of the One giving the message. If our message is condemning, how are we representing the loving Father we are supposedly speaking on behalf of? How will people feel loved if they are afraid to hear from God? Worse yet, are we confirming that God is angry with them by what we share with others "prophetically"?

If you choose to speak, you're also responsible for how and when you speak.
—1 Corinthians 14:32 (The Message)

Imagine that I was to serve you a steak dinner with all the trimmings. Once you're seated, I give you a choice: one of the steaks is presented on a plate of fine china, and the other is presented on a garbage pail lid. Which would you choose?

Generally we would choose the one presented on china. Even though it's the same meal, cooked in the same way, we would tend to want the one served in a desirable fashion. My point is that the way you prophesy is as important as what you prophesy.

Use the prophetic to encourage people, build them up, bring them comfort, and watch God open the doors to the supernatural for you!

The Rest of Sally's Story

As I shared earlier, I came across the stage, and the Lord reminded me of the video I had seen a few weeks earlier of a pastor's wife who had gotten up out of her wheelchair after years of paralysis.

A group of our people had gathered around Sally and were praying for her, shaking heaven's gates on her behalf. My missions pastor, Mohan Maharaj, a man of miracles, was on his knees before Sally, commanding the infirmity in her body to be broken and for God's kingdom to invade her body for total healing. I joined him and all of us together began to command her legs to work in Jesus' name.

Slowly, shakily, Sally stood and began to walk! She walked and walked. She wouldn't stop. Around and around the sanctuary she walked. She wept with joy. We joined her!

The doctors had told her it was over, the physiotherapists had told her it was over, the specialists had told her it was over, but Jesus had another idea.

Sally walked.

My people erupted in praise. Before their eyes, they saw the God of miracles perform a mighty act, and they were a part of it.

We have not been the same. But more importantly, neither has Sally.

That is the power of God at work in people who choose to be naturally supernatural.

Pillar Prayer

Jesus, I thank You that You have given me access to all the power of heaven through the Holy Spirit. I thank You that it is normal for me to live a supernatural lifestyle.

I repent for believing that I am not qualified or able to partner with You in Your power. I choose to break my agreement with powerlessness and fear.

I thank you for risks. I repent for where I have allowed fear to rob me of supernatural opportunities. I am thankful that I am fully empowered to walk naturally supernatural because I can do all things through Christ who strengthens me. In Jesus' name, amen.

Pillar Confession

It is my nature to walk in the nature of my Father (2 Peter 1:4). I am naturally supernatural and I can do all things through Jesus who gives me strength (Philippians 4:13). I choose to engage my faith in the resurrection of Jesus (Romans 4:22–24), and live today for kingdom purposes (Matthew 6:10). I invite divine appointments with the world (Psalm 37:23) to demonstrate God's perfect will to those who are brought into my path (Romans 12:2).

chapter twelve

All Things Are
Possible with God

Jesus looked at them and said, "With man it is impossible, but not with
God. For all things are possible with God."
—Mark 10:27 (emphasis added)

THE GREATEST PROHIBITING FACTOR TO THE BODY OF CHRIST SEEING A
breakthrough in the area of miracles is doubt. Even Mary, the mother of
Jesus, doubted when she was visited by an angel who had a world-chang-
ing message for her.

And Mary said to the angel, "How will this be, since I am a virgin?"
And the angel answered her, "The Holy Spirit will come upon
you, and the power of the Most High will overshadow you; therefore
the child to be born will be called holy—the Son of God. And behold,
your relative Elizabeth in her old age has also conceived a son, and this
is the sixth month with her who was called barren. For nothing will
be impossible with God."
And Mary said, "Behold, I am the servant of the Lord; let it be to
me according to your word." And the angel departed from her.
—Luke 1:34–38 (emphasis added)

Mary's first response was to point out the fact that the Messiah's
birth would be prevented because of an impossibility: she was a virgin.
The angel confirmed his message and encouraged her faith by sharing of

Elizabeth's miracle child. He then makes the wonderful statement that nothing is impossible with God.

Here is where we often get off-track. I'm sure you have heard this saying. Nothing is impossible for God. Conceptually this is true, but the statement kind of leaves us hopeless. While nothing is impossible for Him, we are left in the sorry state of facing impossibility on our own. Though correct in its doctrinal declaration, biblically it is shared a different way.

What Was Saturday Like?

Have you ever wondered what the Saturday was like for the disciples between Good Friday and Resurrection Sunday? Talk about facing impossibility alone. It must have been devastating. They must have felt abandoned and confused.

How do I come to that conclusion? Because of the doubt surrounding Jesus' resurrection.

> *Now it was Mary Magdalene and Joanna and Mary the mother of James and the other women with them who told these things to the apostles,* but these words seemed to them an idle tale, and they did not believe them. *But Peter rose and ran to the tomb; stooping and looking in, he saw the linen cloths by themselves; and he* went home marveling at what had happened.
> —Luke 24:10–12 (emphasis added)

I can't begin to imagine the apostles' desperation. I don't want to judge them, because I would have responded likewise, but it must have been devastating to think that they had given up three years of life to follow a madman or a fraud (so it would have appeared). They would have felt embarrassed, confused, and hopeless.

I asked God about that dark day. In that moment, I felt grace come over my soul, like the Father wrapping me in a blanket of peace, like a child getting wrapped in a warm towel after coming out of a cold lake.

"That's why I only let it be one day," He said. "I knew how hard it would be."

When given the news of the empty tomb, the apostles didn't believe it. Instead they dismissed it as an idle tale. Even though Peter went to the tomb, he didn't come back to declare the truth; rather he went home to think… to wrestle with his doubt.

Jesus did tell them He would rise.

And after flogging him, they will kill him, and on the third day he will rise.

—Luke 18:33

In light of the impossible situation, those words must have become like ash in their mouths.

Doubt is just perverted expectation, the perversion of hope. To be expressed, both doubt and hope need impossibility. Hope is the joyful expectation of good. Doubt is the fearful expectation of bad.

What were the disciples expecting that Saturday? They had been told by Jesus that He would rise. But those words remained empty. Fear would

> Doubt is just perverted expectation, the perversion of hope.

have crept in; wonder as to how they were going to survive the eventual onslaught of the Pharisees; confusion as to how they were going to get their lives back together, or if they ever would. When confronted with the empty tomb, doubt still managed to cloud their faith.

Impossibility will do that. It takes the breath away. There is a sickening finality to impossibility. Any glimmer of hope is extinguished. Doubt gives way to desperation, desperation to hopelessness, and hopelessness to resignation.

It's impossible for a blind eye to see.
It's impossible for a deaf ear to hear.
It's impossible for a lame person to walk.
It's impossible for the dead to rise.

Then we hear the empty promise: nothing is impossible for God. And our reaction is: "Sure, not for God, but certainly for me."

Impossibility provides the atmosphere for the miraculous. We are meant to engage a posture of hope in impossibility, because without impossibility there can be no miracles. However, we aren't meant to engage impossibility by trying to control our doubt; we are meant to engage it from a posture of intimacy.

This chapter's opening scripture doesn't say that all things are possible for God; it says all things are possible *with* God. One little word, one massive shift in understanding.

With comes from the Greek word *para*:

> ...*a primary preposition; properly, near... from beside (literally or figuratively)... at (or in) the vicinity of... to the proximity from, of, at, by, besides, near...*[10]

In other words, it means to be beside, or near. We would look at it as being united to, as in, "I am with you." But this word also means close to or near. What difference does that make?

Glorified Response: Knowing God (Intimacy)

> *"Come, I will send you to Pharaoh that you may bring my people, the children of Israel, out of Egypt." But Moses said to God, "Who am I that I should go to Pharaoh and bring the children of Israel out of Egypt?" He said, "But I will be with you, and this shall be the sign for you, that I have sent you: when you have brought the people out of Egypt, you shall serve God on this mountain."*
> —Exodus 3:10–12 (emphasis added)

---

10 Olive Tree Enhanced Strong's Dictionary, computer software, version 2011, Olive Tree Bible Software, accessed November 3, 2016 (www.olivetree.com).

I once heard a speaker share this passage. He said that Moses was looking for affirmation. Perhaps he was expecting God to say, "You're a great leader, a man of faith and power..." You know, to butter Moses up a little.

Instead God replied by giving the greatest assurance He possibly could: *"I will be with you."*

Moses was looking to be comforted by affirmation, but God gave him something exponentially better. Himself. Moses must have caught on to the value of having God with him, because later he refused to go into the Promised Land without the presence of God.

Imagine it this way. Pluto is a great distance from the sun, approximately 3.5 billion miles. It takes light, which travels at 186,000 miles per second, over five hours to travel from the sun to Pluto. At that distance, it is obviously quite cold there: -380°F. At that temperature, everything is frozen. But if I were able to bring Pluto closer to the sun, everything that is frozen would start to melt—not because the sun had changed, but because of Pluto's proximity to the sun.

Impossibility, like freezing on the sun, doesn't exist for God. Like the possibility of objects on the surface of Pluto melting, the closer I get to God, the less likely impossibility can exist. In other words, as I get closer to Him, my environment has to yield to the condition of His environment. The heat of His power melts away the ice of impossibility.

Alone

Earlier I discussed the importance of being in agreement when establishing a stronghold. In impossibility, the enemy uses hopelessness to get us to agree with the lie that we have been abandoned, that God has abandoned us and left us to our own devices to deal with our circumstances. Not only is deliverance a pipedream, but He is no longer willing to be with us. In that dark place, since we believe the Comforter has left us, we look for any source of comfort. That's the point of hopelessness.

Maybe you are in a dark season of the soul right now. Take courage: you have not been abandoned; you have been invited.

For the Lord will not forsake his people; he will not abandon his heritage.
—Psalms 94:14

The Invitation

Every impossibility is an invitation to greater intimacy. It's like the Father saying, "Is it cold out there in the impossible? Come closer to Me."

> *Let your reasonableness be known to everyone. The Lord is at hand; do not be anxious about anything, but in* everything by prayer and supplication with thanksgiving *let your requests be made known to God.* And the peace of God, which surpasses all understanding, *will guard your hearts and your minds in Christ Jesus.*
> —Philippians 4:5–7 (emphasis added)

My friend Trevor Meier says that to access the peace of God that surpasses understanding, you have to be willing to give up your desire to understand.

Let me put it this way. The impossible is not meant to be understood; it is meant to be overcome. In the same way as impossibility is an invitation to greater intimacy, unanswered prayer holds the same invitation. When you don't get what you're asking for, you get to have more of Jesus.

What if rather than disappointment, you responded to unanswered prayer with an expectation of greater relationship with Jesus? Perhaps we would access surpassing peace.

The Connection: The Resurrection of the Dead

This pillar is connected to the elementary doctrine of the resurrection of the dead. The impossibility of the dead being raised is the ultimate expression of God's miraculous omnipotence. That this incredible miracle is an elementary doctrine points to the fact that it mustn't be overly complicated. However, in the time since the church of Acts, the miraculous has been made complicated indeed. Today's doctrines say that miraculous signs and wonders died with the apostles. That would point to a changing God, which is a frightening thought. If that were true, what else has He changed?

But thanks be to God, He doesn't change.

Every good gift and every perfect gift is from above, coming down from the Father of lights, with whom there is no variation or shadow due to change.

—James 1:17

God hasn't changed His commitment to His children to work miraculously on their behalf. He remains the God with whom all things are possible.

The doctrine of resurrection also affects our faith.

Then the disciples came to Jesus privately and said, "Why could we not cast it out?"

He said to them, "Because of your little faith. For truly, I say to you, if you have faith like a grain of mustard seed, you will say to this mountain, 'Move from here to there,' and it will move, and nothing will be impossible for you."

—Matthew 17:19–20

I'm sure there were times when Jesus drove the disciples crazy. Some of the things He said had to be so confusing. The story in Matthew 17 is one of those moments. What makes it confusing is that a mustard seed is really small. In effect, Jesus was saying, "Because of your little faith... all you need is a little faith."

I'm sure the disciples looked at each other, wondering what they were supposed to do with that. Frankly, I think we feel the same way.

Both Matthew and Mark record this moment. Jesus had come down from being transfigured to find His disciples trying to cast out a demon. Matthew revealed Jesus' interaction with the disciples, but Mark's record gives us a hint as to what Jesus was saying when He spoke of little faith versus the faith of a mustard seed.

And Jesus asked his father, "How long has this been happening to him?"

And he said, "From childhood. And it has often cast him into fire and into water, to destroy him. But if you can do anything, have compassion on us and help us."

And Jesus said to him, "'If you can'! All things are possible for one who believes."

Immediately the father of the child cried out and said, "I believe; help my unbelief!"

—Mark 9:21–24

The same word used for little faith, *apistia*, is used for unbelief.

...faithlessness... disbelief (lack of Christian faith), or...unfaithfulness (disobedience):— unbelief... unfaithfulness, faithless want of faith, unbelief weakness of faith...[11]

The father's cry—*"I believe; help my unbelief!"*—is often the same as our cries. When Jesus referred to little faith, He was referring to a lack of faith, or unbelief. So when Jesus corrected His disciples, He was challenging the location of their faith and calling it what it really was: unbelief. They were putting their faith in the outcome, not in Jesus.

Conversely, the father, when rebuked by Jesus, said the opposite. Jesus rebuked him by saying an incredulous, "If you can!" The father then cried out that he believed in Jesus but was struggling to believe for the outcome.

When our faith is in the outcome, we tend to think we have to muster up enough of it to impress God into responding favourably to our prayer. That's not faith, just positive thinking. Faith is never rooted in the outcome; it is rooted in the person of Jesus. That's why it can be the size of a mustard seed—not emotional, not conditional, but literally based on fact.

The centurion knew it. We see Jesus marvel at his faith in Luke 7:

---

11 Olive Tree Enhanced Strong's Dictionary, computer software, version 2011, Olive Tree Bible Software, accessed November 3, 2016 (www.olivetree.com).

Now Jesus started on His way with them; and when He was not far from the house, the centurion sent friends, saying to Him, "Lord, do not trouble Yourself further, for I am not worthy for You to come under my roof; for this reason I did not even consider myself worthy to come to You, but just say the word, and my servant will be healed. For I also am a man placed under authority, with soldiers under me; and I say to this one, 'Go!' and he goes, and to another, 'Come!' and he comes, and to my slave, 'Do this!' and he does it."

Now when Jesus heard this, He marveled at him, and turned and said to the crowd that was following Him, "I say to you, not even in Israel have I found such great faith.*"*

—Luke 7:6–9, NASB (emphasis added)

The centurion put his faith in Jesus, not the outcome. He saw the authority of Jesus and his faith responded to the authority of Jesus.

What's wonderful about this posture of faith is that it doesn't put the focus on the problem or outcome, but on Jesus alone. When we force ourselves to be positive, and call it faith, we are actually in unbelief.

Belief in an outcome isn't faith; it is belief in the one who brings the outcome. This posture also protects our faith from the outcome. When my faith is in the outcome, I'm left responsible to deal with the mystery of unanswered prayer, causing my faith to suffer. Belief in an outcome isn't faith; faith is belief in the One who brings the outcome.

Paul helps us define this in Romans 4 by speaking of Abraham's faith and how his faith relates to ours.

He did not weaken in faith when he considered his own body, which was as good as dead (since he was about a hundred years old), or when he considered the barrenness of Sarah's womb. No unbelief made him waver concerning the promise of God, but he grew strong in his faith as he gave glory to God, fully convinced that God was able to do what he had promised. That is why his faith was "counted to him as righteousness."
But the words "it was counted to him" were not written for his sake alone, but for ours also. It will be counted to us who

believe in him who raised from the dead Jesus our Lord, *who was delivered up for our trespasses and raised for our justification.*
—Romans 4:19–25 (emphasis added)

Faith is rooted in Jesus, but how does it get lived out?

Renovated Thought: I Possess the Faith I Need

In reference to the righteousness given to us when we believe in the resurrection of Jesus, Paul writes, *"It will be counted to us who believe in him who raised from the dead Jesus our Lord"* (Romans 4:24).

This business of trying to conjure up enough positivity about the outcome is exhausting. It leaves us wondering how much faith will be enough to get God's attention. It leads to a performance-based mindset of prayer and operates in works, not rest.

It doesn't promote intimacy with Jesus; it affirms performing for Him. It makes faith a currency, and if you present enough of it, you will be answered—as if you can purchase an answer from God, when in truth the promises of God were purchased for you.

I'll Believe It When I See It

I'm sure you've heard this saying before: "I'll believe it when I see it." Miracles are a result of our faith; they do not author it. Faith that's based on miraculous outcomes is shallow and will falter if the desired outcome isn't achieved.

> ...*looking to* Jesus, the founder and perfecter of our faith, *who for the joy that was set before him endured the cross, despising the shame, and is seated at the right hand of the throne of God.*
> —Hebrews 12:2 (emphasis added)

How did Jesus both found and perfect our faith? Through His perfect life, death, and resurrection. In other words, if you believe in the gospel, the salvation message, you possess the faith you need. It may seem small, like a mustard seed, but it is great faith. It is the simple belief in Him who raised Jesus from the dead. If you can believe that Jesus died and rose again for your salvation, you possess the faith you need to move mountains!

This connects us to the debit card example I used in Chapter Three. Rather than trying to muster up enough faith, we need to anchor our faith in the work of the resurrection of Christ. Be free from the bondage of not having enough faith and remind yourself of the basis of your salvation, the resurrection. Then attack the impossible!

> *If you can believe that Jesus died and rose again for your salvation, you possess the faith you need to move mountains!*

For the Son of God, Jesus Christ, whom we proclaimed among you, Silvanus and Timothy and I, was not Yes and No, but in him it is always Yes. For all the promises of God find their Yes in him. That is why it is through him that we utter our Amen to God for his glory.

—2 Corinthians 1:19–20 (emphasis added)

Jesus, through His death and resurrection, put us in the Yes of God. All that He has promised is now ours for the receiving. Nothing is withheld. Nothing is out of reach. All that is of God is available to us through Christ!

Truly then, all things are possible with Him!

Pillar Prayer

Father, I thank You that with You all things are possible. I thank You that my circumstances, no matter the impossibilities, are not too big for me when I am with You.

I repent for doubting that You are with me. And I thank You that the work of the cross completes the release of all Your promises to me.

I repent for little faith, and I choose to anchor my faith in Jesus.
Thank You, Jesus, for both founding and perfecting my faith. My faith
in the power of your resurrection makes my faith perfect and adequate.
I thank You that You have given me the faith I need through Jesus.
I command my mountains to be removed from me in Jesus' name. I love
and worship You, my wonderful Saviour. In Your name I pray, amen.

Pillar Confession

I anchor my faith in the complete work of the resurrection of Jesus (Philippians 3:10, Romans 4:22–24). His love for me (Psalm 86:13, Psalm 117, Ephesians 2:4–5) positions me for intimacy with Him and His defeat of death enables me to overcome the impossible (Ephesians 2:6–7, 1 John 4:4, Romans 8:37). All things are possible near Him (Matthew 19:26).

chapter thirteen

God is Good

THIS PILLAR WAS BROUGHT INTO CLARITY FOR ME THROUGH THE MINISTRY OF
Bethel in Redding, California. Bill Johnson's leadership and revelatory
thought toward this truth has shaped so much of my understanding of
the goodness of God.

In Matthew 6, the disciples asked Jesus to teach them to pray. Jesus' response in this powerful moment was to give mankind a pattern for
prayer that has shaped our relationship with God ever since.

> *Pray then like this: "Our Father in heaven, hallowed be your name.*
> *Your kingdom come, your will be done, on earth as it is in heaven.*
> *Give us this day our daily bread, and forgive us our debts, as we also*
> *have forgiven our debtors. And lead us not into temptation, but deliver*
> *us from evil.*
>
> —Matthew 6:9–13

Jesus starts this iconic prayer in an amazing fashion. The Jews of
the day considered God so holy that they'd leave out the vowels when
writing His name, out of reverence for His holiness. But Jesus starts our
prayer by telling us that God's preferred way of being addressed and
viewed is as Father.

Religion, however, has taught us that God is distant and angry, that
the sin of the world has left Him offended at mankind. For more years than
I would like to admit, I had an incomplete view of Jesus as my mediator.

For there is one God, and there is one mediator between God and men, *the man Christ Jesus, who gave himself as a ransom for all, which is the testimony given at the proper time.*

—1 Timothy 2:5–6 (emphasis added)

My perspective was of an angry God looking down at me from heaven, ready to let loose His fiery wrath on me on account of my sin. Then Jesus would step in the way with His hands up and shout, "God, remember that I paid for Landen's sin. Don't destroy him. I have taken care of it." God would reluctantly put down His lightning bolt, but give me this look that would say, "Boy, you are lucky that Jesus stepped in right there or you would have been finished."

Any time I tried to repent of my stuff, my fear of an angry God overwhelmed me. I lived afraid of offending Him and was certainly tricked into being afraid of coming to Him.

This dysfunctional view of God was broken with a revelation that He gave me with one of my daughters. My wife Cathy and I have four amazing kids. In our second ministry assignment, we were in charge of an incredible ministry called Eagles Nest Ranch. Over our seven summers there, we saw thousands of kids and teens impacted with the love of Jesus. Our property was nestled in the Cypress Hills of southern Alberta, near Medicine Hat, and it was the most perfect setting to raise our young family.

In preparing for our summer camp, I had a staff of about one hundred young adults. We would have a week of staff training every year. I would meet daily with our twenty directors to discuss the day and prepare the facilities for the arrival of the kids.

One midmorning, during one of those meetings, my wife came in and asked me if I had seen our third daughter, Amy-Lynn, who was three at the time. I told her that I hadn't but that she was probably playing somewhere and would turn up soon. Cathy went to go look for her and I continued my meeting.

About forty-five minutes later, Cathy interrupted the meeting again, quite frantic this time, saying that she had searched everywhere and couldn't find Amy.

While the ranch was made for kids, it was located in real wilderness. Dense forest surrounded us, and the majority of our seven hundred acres was unbroken backcountry. It wouldn't be hard for a three-year-old to get lost forever in those woods.

We immediately stopped the meeting and the entire staff started to search the grounds.

As a parent, I don't think there's a more terrifying feeling than a missing child. All of the worst fears go through your mind. The ferocity of the emotions are overwhelming, and they all happen at once.

I took one of our ATVs and began to drive around our property, calling out for Amy. Our facilities were in a valley and the pasture land for our horses was at the top of the valley. I drove up there to look for Amy. I called and called for her, getting more and more frantic by the minute. At one point I drove to a familiar spot that overlooked our land where I could see for miles. This normally beautiful sight left me in tears. I remember praying, "Lord, our land is so big and Amy is so small."

After another forty-five minutes of driving trails and calling for her, the longest forty-five minutes of my life, I came back down to our facility. To my absolute relief, there she was, hand-in-hand with one of my staffers, Ben. He had found her in the woods near the horse corral. She had never been more than fifty yards in the woods.

I jumped off the ATV and ran to her.

Now, in the whole time I had searched for her, I never thought about being angry for the way she had filled her diapers. I never once thought about how she would put her hands on her hips and say "No!" Never once did I think about messes she had made or sleepless nights she had caused. I only thought of her beautiful smile, her eyes, the way she would hold my face in her tiny hands and give me kisses. All I could think of were the many, many things I loved about her... and that I could lose all that I loved.

I jumped off the ATV and ran to her. I knelt down and she ran into my arms. I kissed her and hugged her, so thankful we had found her.

Then I asked her, "Amy, Daddy was calling and calling. Didn't you hear me?"

Her answer broke my heart and revealed a stronghold fear I had with God. She said, "I heard you, Daddy, but I thought you were angry, so I was afraid."

God Isn't Angry

In *The Power of the Blood Covenant*, author Malcolm Smith uses two biblical examples to help us understand the nature of the covenant we are in with God.[12] This helps us to understand what the Mediator really did. Both examples occur in the life of David.

The first is when David faced Goliath. Goliath called for the hiding Israelites to send out a champion. If Goliath won, Israel would be enslaved to the Philistines. Should the Hebrew champion win, the Philistines would be Israel's slaves.

Goliath was the Philistines' representative. And upon hearing the taunts of the giant, David asked to represent Israel.

For the Israelite soldiers it must have been terrifying. Every man, woman, and child's destiny, their victory or potential slavery, was represented in David. He was carrying all of Israel's future in his victory or defeat. I wonder how they felt as he slowly began to whirl his sling, knowing their lives and their families' lives were all held in a teenager's hand.

We know what happens. The giant falls, and David, using Goliath's own sword, hacks off the giant's head and holds it up for both armies to see his victory. Suddenly, emboldened by the victory, the armies of Israel swarmed over the embankments and charged into their victory, but Smith adds this thought: it was a victory in which the only thing they had brought to the battle was six weeks of cowardice.

Yet the victory was theirs because their representative won the battle.

The second of Smith's examples is when David honoured his covenant with Jonathan in finding Jonathan's son Mephibosheth.

Shortly before his death, Jonathan and David made a covenant to ensure that there would always be peace and love between their descendants. The covenant was unnecessary for David and Jonathan, because

---

12 Malcolm Smith, *The Power of the Blood Covenant* (Tulsa, OK: Harrison House, 2006).

they loved each other. But when they were gone, their children would need the covenant to remind them how to treat each other's households.

Soon after, Jonathan and his father Saul were killed in battle and David ascended to the throne of Israel. News of Saul's and Jonathan's death sent Jonathan's household into panic. Not knowing David's covenant with Jonathan, his household rushed to hide Jonathan's children. In that day, any new king's first order of business was to destroy the former royal line so that his right to the throne couldn't be challenged by anyone of the former royal lineage.

In the panic, Jonathan's young son Mephibosheth was carried out of the house by a nurse. As she ran, she dropped him, permanently injuring his legs and leaving him lame. They took him away and hid him in a place called Lo Debar, where he grew up. Mephibosheth would have had teachers who told him that he should live in the royal palaces, that it was his birthright to be royal, and that David would kill him if he ever found him.

Years later, David asked if there was anyone left from the house of Jonathan. He heard of Mephibosheth and ordered him to be brought to the palace. Mephibosheth would have thought this was it, that David had found the last in the royal line and would kill him. He was unaware of the covenant that had existed between his father and David.

David, upon seeing Mephibosheth, brought him into the palace, restored all of his lands, and invited him to eat at the king's table for the rest of his days. David delighted in Mephibosheth as if he was Jonathan.

These two examples help us to understand the nature of God and Jesus, the New Covenant mediator.

Firstly, we were in Jesus on the cross. He represented us. His death is ours. His victory is ours. Through our baptism, we are united with His death and resurrection. As I have said before, Jesus took the cross and we take a bath.

But secondly, like David with Mephibosheth, Smith writes that God delights in us like He delights in Jesus. Jesus isn't standing in the way between us and God. He *is* the way, the truth, and the life and we come to the Father by Him!

You are not in the line of fire of
an angry God. The Father, your Father, delights in you like He delights
in Jesus. You are now the object of His
rapt attention, affection, and blessing.

> The Father, your Father,
> delights in you like He
> delights in Jesus.

God is not angry!

The Character of God

Generally, the power of God isn't in question in our lives. We don't
struggle with the concept of whether or not He can do something. More
often than not, the question is whether He will do something. It becomes
a question of His character.

We have been programmed to question the character of God. It's
the first and best lie the enemy has used on mankind ever since Adam and
Eve were in the Garden.

At the root of every lie the enemy sows in our lives, we can see this
questioning of His character: He is not who He says He is.

> *Now the serpent was more crafty than any other beast of the field that
> the Lord God had made.*
>
> *He said to the woman, "Did God actually say, 'You shall not
> eat of any tree in the garden'?"*
>
> *And the woman said to the serpent, "We may eat of the fruit of
> the trees in the garden, but God said, 'You shall not eat of the fruit of
> the tree that is in the midst of the garden, neither shall you touch it, lest
> you die.'"*
>
> *But the serpent said to the woman,* "You will not surely die.
> For God knows that when you eat of it your eyes will be
> opened, and you will be like God, *knowing good and evil.*"
>
> —Genesis 3:1–5 (emphasis added)

In Satan's first attempt to separate man from God, he made them
question God's character. In essence, he said to them that God was

holding something back from them, that He wasn't as He appeared. In so doing, Satan deceived man into independence, and left a looming question over creation: is God good?

Jesus... What You See Is What You Get

Long ago, at many times and in many ways, God spoke to our fathers by the prophets, but in these last days he has spoken to us by his Son, whom he appointed the heir of all things, through whom also he created the world. He [Jesus] is the radiance of the glory of God and the exact imprint of his nature, *and he upholds the universe by the word of his power. After making purification for sins, he sat down at the right hand of the Majesty on high, having become as much superior to angels as the name he has inherited is more excellent than theirs.*

—Hebrews 1:1–4 (emphasis added)

The writer of Hebrews points to Jesus as the exact imprint of God the Father's nature. Jesus challenged Philip in the same fashion.

Jesus said to him, "I am the way, and the truth, and the life. No one comes to the Father except through me. If you had known me, you would have known my Father also. *From now on you do know him and have seen him."*

Philip said to him, "Lord, show us the Father, and it is enough for us." Jesus said to him, "Have I been with you so long, and you still do not know me, Philip? Whoever has seen me has seen the Father. *How can you say, 'Show us the Father'? Do you not believe that* I am in the Father and the Father is in me? *The words that I say to you I do not speak on my own authority, but the Father who dwells in me does his works. Believe me that I am in the Father and the Father is in me, or else believe on account of the works themselves.*

—John 14:6–11 (emphasis added)

Believers cannot create an impression of the character of God that doesn't match the revelation of Jesus.

Jesus gives us a perfect picture of the Father. The way Jesus responds, loves, speaks, and acts gives us a complete revelation of the Father. Bill Johnson has said that Jesus is perfect theology, and in the revelation of the Father, Jesus gives us a perfect theological view of the character of the Father. Therefore, believers cannot create an impression of the character of God that doesn't match the revelation of Jesus.

The Old and New Testament Dichotomy

You might be thinking right now, *Wait a minute, this Father you're describing... I don't see Him in the Old Testament. I see a God of wrath.* For the sake of our conversation, let's refer to the Old Testament as the Old Covenant, and the New Testament, the New Covenant.

One of Satan's last ditch efforts is to trick mankind into thinking that God has changed. This is the great illusion of hell, that God somehow changed when Jesus died and rose again, becoming this loving Father, formerly wanting vengeance for sin but now overlooking it.

The lie is that God was always like He is represented in the Old Covenant. Then suddenly He had a change of heart in the New Covenant. We are tricked into believing that God is the Old Covenant representation of His character for eternity before Christ showed up on the scene.

Black Spot Theology

The way for us to break free from this lie is to learn the truth of the full nature of God.

Imagine an abstract painting, with beautiful colours and shapes. This painting represents God in His eternal existence outside of time and space, and it represents His nature in all its beauty, mystery, and harmony.

Now, look at the painting and notice that there's a small black spot on it, big enough to see but too small to change the flow of the painting. If the whole painting represents the eternal existence and nature of God, this little black spot represents a moment in His existence where sin entered the picture without an adequate covenant to address it.

Said another way, God has always been the revelation of the New Covenant; He hasn't changed. But there was a moment when an inadequate covenant, the Old Covenant (the black spot), covered for sin but didn't eradicate its severity. God was left to respond to mankind in light of the severity of sin. Now, because of the cross, He is now able to respond to sin in His full nature.

Just as Mephibosheth discovered that David wasn't a murderer, so we now can see through Jesus the full nature of our Heavenly Father.

This, however, doesn't negate God's judgement on sin. Rather, through Jesus mankind is given an escape clause from that judgement. That is why God's legal wrath on sin can remain and the fullness of His grace towards sinful mankind can be expressed, placing us in the favourable condition of having this powerful covenant of the cross working on our behalf for salvation.

Minimum Payments

For since the law has but a shadow of the good things to come instead of the true form of these realities, it can never, by the same sacrifices that are continually offered every year, make perfect those who draw near. Otherwise, would they not have ceased to be offered, since the worshipers, having once been cleansed, would no longer have any consciousness of sins? But in these sacrifices there is a reminder of sins every year. For it is impossible for the blood of bulls and goats to take away sins.

Consequently, when Christ came into the world, he said, "Sacrifices and offerings you have not desired, but a body have you prepared for me; in burnt offerings and sin offerings you have taken no pleasure. Then I said, 'Behold, I have come to do your will, O God, as it is written of me in the scroll of the book.'"

When he said above, "You have neither desired nor taken pleasure in sacrifices and offerings and burnt offerings and sin offerings" (these are offered according to the law), then he added, "Behold, I have come to do your will." He does away with the first in order to establish the second. And by that will we have been sanctified through the offering of the body of Jesus Christ once for all.

—Hebrews 10:1–10 (emphasis added)

Think of the Old Covenant like a bad debt, a debt that's too large to pay off. Because of its size, we maintain it by making the minimum monthly payments, basically paying interest on the debt and never seeing the principle reduced.

The Old Covenant dealt with sin as a bad debt. Bulls and lambs were only the minimum payment. They covered the sin, but did not pay the debt.

The problem with believing the lie that God has changed is that it reduces the cross to a minimum payment, leading Christians to believe that the sacrifice of Jesus is like the blood of bulls and lambs covering sin, but God's offence against man's sin still remains. Fear enters the picture when believers are duped into thinking that perhaps God actually is still the character in the black spot stories, leaving us to fear that perhaps He hasn't changed from the black spot. By trying to be good believers throughout pious living and good works, we think that somehow we're making minimum payments on that offence so that God will suspend His righteous judgement against us.

In truth, the sacrifice of Jesus fully paid the debt of sin. As the writer of Hebrews declared, we have been sanctified once and for all through the offering of the body of Jesus Christ. That sacrifice allows for mankind to engage God not from a debtor's condition but freed of the debt. We can relate to Him in His true nature.

God is good. The Old Covenant reality, the black spot, was a moment in history, not the eternal condition of our great God.

The Connection

This pillar is connected to the elementary doctrine of faith toward God. When we come to grips with His nature, and understand that He isn't changing, rather than running from Him we can run to Him. But as long as fear dictates our response to God's character, we'll be lost in the confusion of whether or not it is safe to approach Him.

> *Since then we have a great high priest who has passed through the heavens, Jesus, the Son of God, let us hold fast our confession. For we do not have a high priest who is unable to sympathize with our weaknesses, but one who in every respect has been tempted as we are, yet without sin.* Let us then with confidence draw near to the throne of grace, *that we may receive mercy and find grace to help in time of need.*
> —Hebrews 4:14–16 (emphasis added)

Glory to God! Because of Jesus, we can boldly draw near to the throne of grace.

Glorified Response: Having Confidence in His Character (Truth)

> *As for the word that he sent to Israel, preaching good news of peace through Jesus Christ (he is Lord of all), you yourselves know what happened throughout all Judea, beginning from Galilee after the baptism that John proclaimed: how God anointed Jesus of Nazareth with the Holy Spirit and with power.* He went about doing good and healing all who were oppressed by the devil, for God was with him.
> —Acts 10:36–38 (emphasis added)

Earlier in the chapter, we came to understand that Jesus is the perfect representation of the Father. This pillar is one of the most difficult to come to grips with, especially when we see the evil in the world or when we don't see a breakthrough in our prayers. The question of God's goodness is, I believe, one of our biggest prohibiting factors from expressing the miraculous in this time of history.

It wasn't until this was settled in my heart that I began to see a breakthrough of healing in my ministry. Since recalibrating my heart towards His goodness, I no longer wrestle with whether or not it is God's will to heal.

I still hear statement like, "God gave me this sickness" or "God is teaching me something through this." Acts 10:36–38 says that Jesus went about doing good. In the context of scripture, do you see Jesus making people sick so He can make them better? Do you see Jesus stopping his prayers for someone and saying, "My Father is trying to teach you something. That's why He gave this to you"? When He raised people from the dead, did he chastise them for their lack of faith?

No.

I would be put in jail if I injured my kids because I liked nursing them back to health. That isn't loving; it is abusive. God doesn't give sickness and disease. He doesn't hurt His kids so that He can heal them. He is good, He is good all the time, and there is no shifting of shadow in His nature.

I grow weary of Satan hitting people with sickness or trials and then running away yelling that God did it.

Two Job Descriptions

When my mind was in the process of being renovated on this subject, I heard Bill Johnson share that there are two cosmic job descriptions given by Jesus with regard to the difference between Him and the devil.

> *The thief comes only to steal and kill and destroy. I came that they may have life and have it abundantly.*
>
> —John 10:10

We have the thief—Satan. His job description is to steal, kill, and destroy.

Then we have Jesus. His job description is to bring life and life abundantly.

Look at the issue from the perspective of the job description. The words sickness, disease, and trauma sound similar to steal, kill, and destroy. That makes it pretty easy to discern who's behind it.

God Doesn't Gamble

I heard Danny Silk once say that the reason we have a hard time comprehending the ways of God is that we don't have an experiential frame of reference for the thought that God has never been afraid. This is hard for us to comprehend because we face fear daily. But God has never dealt with fear, because He has never been scared by anything.

It's important to grasp this when we look at Him through tough circumstances. He is never intimidated or afraid of anything. Cancer doesn't frighten Him. Trauma doesn't faze Him. He cannot and will not respond in fear to anything, for there is no fear in Him; He is perfect love, and perfect love casts out all fear (1 John 4:18).

He never *hopes* that things will turn out okay. He *wills* it.

And we know that for those who love God all things work together for good, *for those who are called according to his purpose.*
—Romans 8:28 (emphasis added)

Bill Johnson has also said that God doesn't bring us pain, but He is so good at fixing things that it looks like He did it in the first place.

The words "work" and "good" in Romans 8:28 imply positive synergy. God causes a synergy between all things so that we can gain maximum benefit. But for that to happen, we must be in a mindset of His goodness or we will abort the blessing that could come our way.

While it could appear that God is gambling, nothing is left to chance with Him. He has determined that everything in our lives can benefit us should we trust Him.

Renovated Thought: I Can Trust Him

Once the issue of His character is settled in our minds, we can truly engage faith. James writes to the body of Christ of being settled in our minds:

If any of you lacks wisdom, let him ask God, who gives generously to all without reproach, and it will be given him. But let him ask in faith, with no doubting, for the one who doubts is like a wave of the sea that is driven and tossed by the wind. *For that person must not suppose that he will receive anything from the Lord;* he is a double-minded man, unstable in all his ways.

—James 1:5–8 (emphasis added)

This singlemindedness will help is gain wisdom when we walk through difficult circumstances, helping us not to abandon His goodness in the hope of gaining understanding.

Mystery and Victory

There was a wonderful young family in our church with three beautiful kids. One day, the young dad took me out for coffee and told me some terrible news. He had been diagnosed with a cancerous brain tumour.

We fought hard for this family. I watched his lovely young wife take care of him in the hospital; many of us went in regularly to visit and pray for him. We fasted and prayed. We laid hands on him at every turn, declaring the goodness of God and commanding the tumour to die. Our faith never wavered and we didn't give up. He never wavered in his faith either.

Sadly, we lost that battle and the young dad went home to be with Jesus.

That was a hard loss on our church family. We were so confident that he would be healed and we were devastated.

Dealing with the mystery of unanswered prayer is difficult. We are emotionally invested in those we pray for, and we feel like we deserve an explanation when our prayers aren't answered. But there is a peace that overrides our understanding when we choose by faith to trust God in the midst of the mystery.

This is one of the necessary tensions that the naturally supernatural believer must face: the willingness to face the impossible with unwavering faith and trust in God, regardless of the outcome. It isn't all glorious, and there is great pain associated with the disappointment of not seeing the breakthrough you desire. But being willing to mourn with those who mourn and rejoice with those who rejoice (Romans 12:15) is the part of the believer's suffering that Paul speaks of in Romans 8.

It may seem irresponsible to label the loss of that young dad as a mystery and move on. But that is part of the covenant privilege we walk in. We know that God is good and that all will work out in our favour. We don't need an explanation from God or for anyone.

Dr. Randy Clark is a world leader in the realm of healing ministry. In his school of healing, he shares a message called "The Thrill of Victory and the Agony of Defeat" in which he relates painful stories of times when he had to accept the mystery of God.

Both Randy Clark and Bill Johnson teach about the mountain of faith in Hebrews 11, and I would like to take a moment to look at that scripture, and what both Randy and Bill have taught, to help us navigate through mystery.

Hebrews 11 is often referred to as the Hall of Faith, which mentions the miraculous breakthroughs experienced by many biblical figures due to their faith. Then the chapter takes a different turn:

And what more shall I say? For time would fail me to tell of Gideon, Barak, Samson, Jephthah, of David and Samuel and the prophets— who through faith conquered kingdoms, enforced justice, obtained promises, stopped the mouths of lions, quenched the power of fire, escaped the edge of the sword, were made strong out of weakness, became mighty in war, put foreign armies to flight. Women received back their dead by resurrection. Some were tortured, refusing to accept release, so that they might rise again to a better life. Others suffered mocking and flogging, and even chains and imprisonment. They were stoned, they were sawn in two, they were killed with the sword. They went about in skins of sheep and goats, destitute, afflicted, mistreated—of whom the world was not worthy—wandering about in deserts and mountains, and in dens and caves of the earth.

And all these, though commended through their faith, did not receive what was promised, since God had provided something better for us, that apart from us they should not be made perfect.

—Hebrews 11:32–40

The writer is still mentioning victories of faith, but the narrative turns at verse 35. Suddenly he's talking about those who were tortured, mocked, flogged, and imprisoned. Many were martyred and lived as nomads.

Hebrews 11 is like a mountain. We ascend toward the summit, hearing of all these great breakthroughs of faith. Then we begin to descend and hear of all the defeats in the context of faith. On the ascent, we read about those who received the promise, and on the descent, according to verse 39, we encounter those who didn't receive their promise. But they were all commended for their faith.

I often feel that the people who receive the answers or miracles have better faith than I do—as if there's some sort of greater value to their story and lives than mine.

Faith that sees the breakthrough holds the same value to God as the faith that hasn't seen the breakthrough yet. This is important. Many people feel that since they haven't had an answer to their prayers, perhaps they hold lesser value to the Lord. Or they feel that somehow those who do receive an answer have found a way to better faith.

But then the writer says something interesting:

And all these, though commended through their faith, did not receive what was promised, since God had provided something better for us, that apart from us they should not be made perfect.
—Hebrews 11:39–40

Is it possible to be in heaven and not be perfect? Those who have gone before us, who haven't seen the breakthrough according to this verse, remain incomplete. How is that better for us, that they should remain incomplete? I think that blessings and rewards continue to be released in heaven to those who by faith didn't see their breakthrough on this side of eternity.

For every breakthrough we have here, I believe that young dad is rewarded for his journey in faith to the end.

God is Good

The Thrill of Victory

God is so good that sometimes He is good even when we aren't asking for it. I once had the joy of travelling with Randy Clark to Brazil on a ministry trip with his organization, Global Awakening. After a service in which we prayed for the sick, a young lady came up to me and pointed to her left eye. Since I don't speak Portuguese, I took her nonverbal cue to pray.

We had been praying for folks for about two hours and I was a little tired, and perhaps a little dense as well. I could see that she had a strong prescription for glasses so I assumed that her left eye was worse than her right eye and that she wanted it to be healed so she could have the same vision in each eye.

I didn't know she was blind in the left eye.

I prayed for her and commanded her eye to be healed. I asked her if she was better and the interpreter who had just joined us got all excited.

"She's fifty percent better," the translator said. I didn't understand why he would be so excited.

Big deal, I thought. *So she's seeing fifty percent less blurry than before.*

I had no idea that she was seeing fifty percent out of that eye for the first time! I prayed for her three more times, and each time she experienced improvement until at the last prayer she was seeing one hundred percent out of the blind eye!

The problem was, I didn't find out until after the meeting! We laughed pretty hard afterwards. This was my first time experiencing God's opening a blind eye… and I hadn't even been praying for it! God is so good that even when you ask wrong, He answers right!

God is good and He is good all the time. You can trust Him in victory and in mystery. He loves you!

Pillar Prayer

I thank You, God, that Jesus perfectly revealed you to me. I thank You that Your heart and thoughts toward me are good and that You delight in me in the same way You delight in Jesus.

I repent for thinking that You would do bad things to me, and I choose today to fully embrace that You are good all the time.

I love You and worship You, for You are a good father. You're my Father, hallowed be your name. I bless your goodness. In Jesus' wonderful name, amen.

Pillar Confession

I confess that my God is good (Psalm 100:5, 118). He is good all the time and He doesn't change (James 1:17). Nothing that I experience today cannot be used by God for my good (Romans 8:28). I trust Him completely (Psalm 9:10, 2 Corinthians 3:4), follow Him wholeheartedly (1 Peter 2:21), partner with Him joyfully (2 Corinthians 6:1 Nehemiah 8:10), and love Him with all my being (Mark 12:30).

chapter fourteen

Final Thoughts

IN CONCLUDING OUR JOURNEY TOGETHER, I WOULD LIKE TO TAKE SOME TIME TO firmly establish the importance of rest in the context of these renovated pillars of thought.

One question still plagued me in my pursuit of the pillars: why did He call them ancient?

I would soon find out.

My staff and I gathered for one of our regular meetings. We often read a chapter of a book and then spent some time discussing what we felt the Lord was saying to us personally and corporately. Sometimes there was nothing, and sometimes amazing discussions arose.

I'm blessed with an incredible team. They are all spiritually astute and seasoned in intercession, discernment, and faith. It is a joy to journey with them. As we discussed the chapter we had just read, which was about grace and works, suddenly one of my staff, who is mature in intercession, began to share a concern about a works mentality that she felt might be infiltrating the minds of our people, like the leaven of the Pharisees.

She'd had a dream a couple of nights previous in which she was in church and so excited about getting clean that she took a scalpel and cut her own abdomen open; she pulled out her insides to wash them so they would be clean. Then I came into the room and was horrified to see what she was doing. In the dream, she began to weep and, in a spirit of intercession, spoke on behalf of our congregation: "Pastor Landen, we trust you and we have come so far, but now I have to build these pillars?

I don't think I have the strength to do anything else. Will I ever arrive at maturity? I'm starting to get discouraged."

My response in her dream revealed that my intent was never for my people to think this way, but of course the enemy will use every opportunity to bring confusion to God's people—and this was one of those times.

Suddenly, others in the meeting began to feel the same intercession and we went before the Lord and repented for not completely engaging all of the revelation of these ancient Pillars, asking God to reveal heaven's perspective on what we needed to do.

I want to look at a couple of instances in Scripture where Jesus confronts the management of revelation.

Earlier, I shared about David and the Millo. David built the city of the Jerusalem from the Millo inward, the point being that we are supposed to build our lives from the strongholds of thought inward. These strongholds are meant to give us the peace of God to guard our hearts and minds.

Again, in my original vision of the pillars, the Lord labelled them as ancient. Why ancient?

After David had reigned in Hebron over Judah for seven years, he and his men fought the Jebusites and took over Jerusalem.

And David lived in the stronghold *and called it the city of David. And David* built the city all around from the Millo inward. *And David became greater and greater, for the Lord, the God of hosts, was with him.*

—2 Samuel 5:9–10 (emphasis added)

David, having conquered Jerusalem, lived within its stronghold. He built the city up afterwards, but where he lived wasn't built by him; he lived in what he hadn't built on his own.

These strongholds were built for us, not by us. Think of it this way:

1. The Old Man Is Dead: Can you put your sin nature to death?
2. Filled with God Himself: Can you fill yourself?

3. Children with an Inheritance: Can you make your own inheritance?

4. Naturally Supernatural: Can you manufacture the supernatural?

5. All Things Are Possible with God: Do you have the power of impossibility?

6. God Is Good: Did you have anything to do with that?

A renovated/renewed mind and transformed life are the covenant privileges of all believers. But our lives are not transformed by the sweat equity of good works, but rather by simply choosing to agree with what heaven has already established as normal. That's how we renovate our thoughts. The reality that we see around us is not the reality of heaven, so it becomes our responsibility as believers to renovate our thinking and then live our lives in the reality heaven provides for us.

> Our lives are not transformed by the sweat equity of good works, but rather by simply choosing to agree with what heaven has already established as normal.

Let me pose a question: were you physically there at the cross when Jesus died? I realize this question could seem a bit silly. I understand the doctrine from the perspective of being represented in Christ, but we weren't physically present. Remember Mephibosheth? The covenant between David and Jonathan existed before Mephibosheth did. He was in the favor of the King before he knew he could have the favor of the King. When Jesus was about to give up His Spirit, He said, "It is finished." He finished the work, overcame sin, and made an atonement on my behalf long before I existed.

It was finished before I started. Think about this truth before we go further. It was finished before I started. The curse of our sin-sick past was demolished before our past even began. *It is finished.* This understanding helps us engage a healthy stewardship of revelation.

When we transitioned from the discipleship portion of the book to the pillars, we looked at Matthew 16 where Peter confessed Jesus as the

Son of God. We talked of how Jesus wasn't establishing the church on Peter but on Peter's confession of Jesus.

I would like to look at Matthew 16 a little further. Jesus starts with a warning to His disciples:

And they began discussing it among themselves, saying, "We brought no bread." But Jesus, aware of this, said, "O you of little faith, why are you discussing among yourselves the fact that you have no bread? Do you not yet perceive? Do you not remember the five loaves for the five thousand, and how many baskets you gathered? Or the seven loaves for the four thousand, and how many baskets you gathered? How is it that you fail to understand that I did not speak about bread? Beware of the leaven of the Pharisees and Sadducees." Then they understood that he did not tell them to beware of the leaven of bread, but of the teaching of the Pharisees and Sadducees.

—Matthew 16:7–12

Beware of the leaven of the Pharisees.

Earlier, we discussed the potential of heaven's kingdom. Like yeast in a lump of dough, it can permeate every aspect of our lives. Those who have embraced a compartmentalized lifestyle cannot fully experience His kingdom come, because they have created areas where the kingdom isn't allowed to be expressed in them.

The enemy has found a way, using the principle of leaven, to counterfeit healthy transformation. The leaven of the Pharisees is religion. We need to heed Jesus' warning that the leaven of religion can pollute the work of God by changing it from an act of worship, from a posture of rest, to a fleshly attempt to earn heaven's attention and favour.

Many are trapped into thinking that the acquisition of knowledge can replace revelation—or worse, that possessing knowledge is transformation. Revelation is not for information but for transformation. It is necessary for us as believers to have an encounter with God that opens our hearts to a revelation that renovates our thinking. One form depends upon a temporal acquisition which leads to learning to do what's right;

the other is a spiritual transformation that results in the fruit of doing right. Massive, massive difference.

In Matthew 16:7–12, Jesus warns the disciples of this leaven and then uses examples of kingdom provision and kingdom principles (loaves and leftovers from two miraculous lunches) to engage the disciples to change the way they think so that they agree with heaven's way. Always remember that trying to gain knowledge that will help you build His kingdom will lead to religion, because you cannot build what is already established.

I'd like to look at another unique perspective of Peter's confession:

Now when Jesus came into the district of Caesarea Philippi, he asked his disciples, "Who do people say that the Son of Man is?"

And they said, "Some say John the Baptist, others say Elijah, and others Jeremiah or one of the prophets."

He said to them, "But who do you say that I am?"

Simon Peter replied, "You are the Christ, the Son of the living God."

And Jesus answered him, "Blessed are you, Simon Bar-Jonah! For flesh and blood has not revealed this to you, but my Father who is in heaven. And I tell you, you are Peter, and on this rock I will build my church, and the gates of hell shall not prevail against it. I will give you the keys of the kingdom of heaven, and whatever you bind on earth shall be bound in heaven, and whatever you loose on earth shall be loosed in heaven." Then he strictly charged the disciples to tell no one that he was the Christ.

—Matthew 16:13–20 (emphasis added)

This wonderful moment is filled with rich truth. Here, Jesus invites the disciples into a revelatory practice. He starts by dividing between sources: *Who do men say that I am?* and *Who do you say that I am?* Interesting. Only one of these sources has any resources.

Let me explain. When Jesus asked who men said He was, He gave the disciples an option to choose a source (men) who would have a resource (knowledge). However, man's knowledge proved incorrect. Men had wrongly identified Jesus as John the Baptist or Elijah. Then Jesus challenged the disciples to go to another source (themselves), without the resource of knowledge, and asked them the same question. *Who do You say that I am?*

That might have felt a little unfair. I can see the disciples looking at each other, thinking, *Why would He ask us that? We're not rabbis. How are we supposed to know?*

Then Peter the impetuous speaks before he thinks—Peter, whose boldness got him into trouble but also gave him experiences that none of the others got. Peter says, *"You are the Christ, the Son of the living God."*

Peter's confession didn't come from him; it came from God. Jesus responded to Peter by declaring him blessed because he'd heard what heaven had said about Jesus and spoke it in agreement. Peter agreed with heaven's perspective of Jesus and declared it. Peter tapped into a resource that was greater than the resources of men.

> *Blessed are you, Simon Bar-Jonah! For flesh and blood has not revealed this to you, but my Father who is in heaven.*
>
> —Matthew 16:17

As Christ followers, we must remember this wonderful fact. When there is no resource, there is the Source. When we come to the end of our resources, understanding, and knowledge of men, we are given the opportunity to discover through faith what our Father wants to reveal to us. You see, man's knowledge will seem reasonable, but revelation from God will point to the supernatural.

When there is no resource, there is the Source.

But it gets even better. As believers mature, they learn to move from seeking earthly knowledge as a first resource to engaging revelation. When I speak of revelation, I'm not speaking of creating extra-biblical interpretations of God's kingdom. Rather, revelation is a fresh understanding of His nature and what He is saying in a moment, which can be confirmed by what He has already said in His Word.

The counterfeit of revelation is found in a scripture we looked at extensively earlier in this book:

Final Thoughts

We destroy arguments and every lofty opinion raised against the knowledge of God, and take every thought captive to obey Christ...

—2 Corinthians 10:5

The word argument comes from the Greek word *logismo*, which can also be rendered as imagination or speculations. Here's the point: the counterfeit to revelation is imagination. How can you tell the difference between the two? Imaginations or speculations will assume that God should somehow fit into your picture for your temporal benefit. Revelation will show you the nature of God and how you fit into His picture for your transformation. In other words, speculation is when we imagine or create a scenario determining what we think God should do for us. Revelation is God revealing who He is to draw us closer to Him, and through that closeness make us look more like Jesus. One gives our circumstance and human reasoning lordship while the other brings us to a greater understanding of His nature and lordship.

The men around Jesus used knowledge and reason to wrongly identify Him, but Peter had a revelation which Jesus confirmed wasn't from flesh and blood but from His Father. Peter's confession unlocked an understanding of who Jesus was that released one of the most important "Thy will be done" moments in history.

Let's look at Jesus' response to Peter's confession:

Blessed are you, Simon Bar-Jonah! For flesh and blood has not revealed this to you, but my Father who is in heaven. And I tell you, you are Peter, and on this rock I will build my church, and the gates of hell shall not prevail against it. I will give you the keys of the kingdom of heaven, and whatever you bind on earth shall be bound in heaven, and whatever you loose on earth shall be loosed in heaven."

—Matthew 16:17–19

Pretty heady stuff—a name change and a declaration of destiny and purpose. But Peter, impulsive Peter, didn't heed Jesus' prior warning about the leaven of the Pharisees. He models for us a mistake that many of us unknowingly make which leads us into great bondage.

*From that time Jesus began to show his disciples that he must go to Je-
rusalem and suffer many things from the elders and chief priests and
scribes, and be killed, and on the third day be raised. And Peter took
him aside and began to rebuke him, saying, "Far be it from you, Lord!
This shall never happen to you." But he turned and said to Peter, "Get
behind me, Satan! You are a hindrance to me. For you are not setting
your mind on the things of God, but on the things of man."*

—Matthew 16:21–23

Peter, with newfound confidence in the importance of his recent
promotion, speaks into Jesus' plans, only to be quickly demoted. Actually, a meteoric drop in position! Just a moment ago, Jesus was talking
about the church being built on this rock, Peter, and keys and gates and
binding and loosing... and now Jesus equates Peter to Satan. I can only
imagine the varied emotions Peter must have felt in that moment, and
I'm sure confusion was one of them.

Peter's downfall happened because he thought he had something
to do with establishing the church that Jesus declared hell would not
withstand.

We can have this wonderful open heaven reality, but if we think we
can obtain it by fleshly means, we are deceived into a religious mindset.
Or, as scripture puts it:

*...having the appearance of godliness, but denying its power. Avoid
such people.*

—2 Timothy 3:5

We must resist the temptation to think that experiencing an open
heaven depends on our works, because then, like Peter, we become an
adversary (Satan) to Jesus. We become a hindrance to what He wants to
do because our minds are set on earthly things and not on heaven.

This beautiful gospel, the good news, is that Jesus represented
mankind for the sake of a covenant, a much better covenant than the
law, being established so that mankind would be the benefactors of that
covenant. We did not earn it, nor did we have the capacity to represent

ourselves in it. The Godhead, in infinite love for us, provided a way through the death and resurrection of Jesus for mankind to know both salvation and infinite love.

With this in mind, we can understand why the kingdom is given as an inheritance and not a wage, and why we are called His children instead of slaves. Sin pays wages, but our great Heavenly Father gives us an inheritance—a rich bounty of grace, love, faith, and power that's earned for us by the work of the cross, and freely given to us from a Father's heart of infinite grace and love.

My sincere desire is that through this book you are able to reign in life as you renovate your mind by learning to think what heaven thinks, and make that the truth you live by, and that you would be able to hide in the strongholds God has provided to us as ancient pillars that hold up an open heaven, and be renovated for glory.

Pillar Confessions

I confess today that my mind is being renewed (Romans 12:2) and that I am learning how heaven thinks and setting my mind on the kingdom of heaven's way (Colossians 3:2).

The Old Man is Dead

My old nature is dead (Romans 6:11). I am united with Jesus in His death and resurrection through my confession of His lordship (Romans 10:9). My baptism forever separated me from my old nature (Romans 6:6–7) and because of God's grace I can live sin-free today (Romans 6:14).

Children with an Inheritance

I am loved by God and I am His child (1 John 3:1). I am purchased by His blood (Ephesians 1:7) and my inheritance is heaven (Ephesians 1:11). Through the gift of the Holy Spirit (Acts 2:38), I have access today to all of the resources of heaven (Ephesians 1:13–14). I am not an orphan (John 14:18). I am adopted and an heir (Romans 8:15–17). Through Jesus I am positioned to receive all blessings—spiritually (Ephesians 1:3), emotionally (Philippians 4:7, Ephesians 3:16–17), and physically— (Matthew 6:25–34, Philippians 4:19) from my Father who is in heaven (Matthew 6:9).

Naturally Supernatural

It is my nature to walk in the nature of my Father (2 Peter 1:4). I am naturally supernatural and can do all things through Jesus who gives me strength (Philippians 4:13). I choose to engage my faith in the resurrection of Jesus (Romans 4:22–24) and live today for kingdom purposes (Matthew 6:10). I invite divine appointments with the world (Psalm 37:23) to demonstrate God's perfect will to those brought into my path (Romans 12:2).

Filled With God Himself

For I am not filled by Him, I am filled with Him (Acts 2:1–4, Ephesians 5:18). The Holy Spirit dwells within me (John 7:38–39, 1 Corinthians 3:16). My free gift from Jesus is the Holy Spirit (Acts 2:38) who enables me (1 Corinthians 12:4–11, Hebrews 2:4) to do every good work He has planned for me this day (Ephesians 2:10).

All Things are Possible with God

I anchor my faith in the complete work of the resurrection of Jesus (Philippians 3:10, Romans 4:22–24). His love for me (Psalm 86:13, Psalm 117, Ephesians 2:4–5) positions me for intimacy with Him, and His defeat of death enables me to overcome the impossible (Ephesians 2:6–7, 1 John 4:4, Romans 8:37). All things are possible near Him (Matthew 19:26).

God is Good

I confess that my God is good (Psalm 100:5, 118). He is good all the time and He doesn't change (James 1:17). Nothing that I experience today cannot be used by God for my good (Romans 8:28). I trust Him completely (Psalm 9:10, 2 Corinthians 3:4), follow Him wholeheartedly (1 Peter 2:21), partner with Him joyfully (2 Corinthians 6:1 Nehemiah 8:10), and love Him with all my being (Mark 12:30).

My mind is made up (Isaiah 50:7), my heart is filled with His goodness (Hebrews 10:22), and my will is submitted to His purpose for this day (Luke 22:42–43). This is His day, He made it, and I will rejoice and be glad in it (Psalm 118:24). This is my confession!

Pillar Prayers

The Old Man is Dead

Father I have believed that sin still has dominion over me. I ask your forgiveness for the believing the lie that the cross didn't cure me. I repent of that mindset and I choose to embrace the truth that my old nature is gone and not a part of me any more. I receive the freedom of my new nature and I declare in Jesus name, MY OLD MAN IS DEAD.

Thank you for my freedom, strengthen my heart to not choose the passions of the flesh and to engage the power of your Spirit.

Thank you for Your love for me. In Jesus' name, amen.

Filled With God Himself

Father, I thank You for Your Holy Spirit and I am asking that You give Him to me as my free gift of salvation. Holy Spirit, I want you to fill me and come into my heart. Baptize me in Your great power and fill me so that torrents of living water flow from me to the world around me. I pray that the world would be drenched with a flood from heaven. I repent for devaluing Your place in my life and heart and choose today for You to lead, guide, and empower me to be a witness for Jesus! I want to be filled with God Himself.

Thank You, Father, for Your lavish gift of the Holy Spirit. Thank You, Jesus, for purchasing my salvation with Your blood to make me a temple for the Holy Spirit. Thank you, Holy Spirit, for filling me and empowering me.

God, I am grateful for Your love. In Jesus' name, amen.

Children with an Inheritance

Father, I thank You that I am adopted. I thank You that You love me extravagantly and that You reward me in the same way. I thank You that I am securely established as Your child and securely established as Your heir. I ask that You renew my mind and establish my understanding in this: I am Your child and You will reward me.

I repent for being short-sighted in my living and in my obedience to You. I choose to say yes to what You are saying yes to, and to live today with eternity in mind.

I thank You that You are rewarding me and that You are going to reward me for my obedience. I pray that I would have an encounter with the kingdom of heaven today.

I thank you that you are a rewarder of those who seek You, and I choose to seek You today. In Jesus' wonderful name, amen.

Naturally Supernatural

Jesus, I thank You that You have given me access to all the power of heaven through the Holy Spirit. I thank You that it is normal for me to live a supernatural lifestyle.

I repent for believing that I am not qualified or able to partner with You in Your power. I choose to break my agreement with powerlessness and fear.

I thank you for risks. I repent for where I have allowed fear to rob me of supernatural opportunities. I am thankful that I am fully empowered to walk naturally supernatural because I can do all things through Christ who strengthens me. In Jesus' name, amen.

Appendix Two: Pillar Prayers

All Things are Possible with God

Father, I thank You that with You all things are possible. I thank You that my circumstances, no matter the impossibilities, are not too big for me when I am with You.

I repent for doubting that You are with me. And I thank You that the work of the cross completes the release of all Your promises to me.

I repent for little faith, and I choose to anchor my faith in Jesus. Thank You, Jesus, for both founding and perfecting my faith. My faith in the power of your resurrection makes my faith perfect and adequate.

I thank You that You have given me the faith I need through Jesus. I command my mountains to be removed from me in Jesus' name. I love and worship You, my wonderful Saviour. In Your name I pray, amen.

God is Good

I thank You, God, that Jesus perfectly revealed you to me. I thank You that Your heart and thoughts toward me are good and that You delight in me in the same way You delight in Jesus.

I repent for thinking that You would do bad things to me, and I choose today to fully embrace that You are good all the time.

I love You and worship You, for You are a good father. You're my Father, hallowed be your name. I bless your goodness. In Jesus' wonderful name, amen.

About the Author

Rev. Landen Dorsch began his first ministry assignment in 1996 in a small church called Gospel Chapel in Sylvan Lake, Alberta. He served as an assistant pastor overseeing worship and youth ministry.

After a healthy and vibrant season of ministry at Gospel Chapel, he and his family embarked upon their second ministry assignment at Eagles Nest Ranch, nestled in the Cypress Hills south of Medicine Hat, Alberta. As executive director, Landen led a team of one hundred staff at the summer camp for at-risk kids and teens. During their summer camping season, Landen and his team used dynamic worship and creative themes and activities to draw youth into a saving knowledge of Jesus. Over the course of his time at Eagles Nest, Landen saw thousands of kids and teens impacted with the gospel.

When his season ended at Eagles Nest Ranch, Landen and his family returned to the Edmonton area, where he grew up, to pastor Gateway Family Church in Leduc. He continues to lead that church at the time of this writing.

Landen has the heart of a worshipper. He is an insightful, anointed communicator and a gifted worship leader with a passion to see God's family enter into His presence. At the core of his ministry, Landen models empowerment and pursues the facilitation of the destiny of those he leads. With a message of hope, Landen challenges and encourages the body of Christ to enter into the fullness of what God's Kingdom has to offer.

Landen and his wife Cathy have for children—Alyssa, Tyler, Amy-Lynn, and Jenna. As a family, they are all committed to see God's kingdom advance through themselves and those they lead. He and his family love to laugh and enjoy being in Christ-centred community.

For more information, or to contact Landen
or Gateway, visit their website:
www.gatewayfamily.ca